United States Government Accountability Office

Report to Congressional Requesters

I0411555

September 2014

SECURE FLIGHT

TSA Should Take Additional Steps to Determine Program Effectiveness

GAO Highlights

Highlights of GAO-14-531, a report to congressional requesters

SECURE FLIGHT

TSA Should Take Additional Steps to Determine Program Effectiveness

Why GAO Did This Study

In 2009, DHS's TSA began using Secure Flight to screen passengers against high-risk lists. These lists, subsets of the TSDB—the U.S. government's consolidated list of known and suspected terrorists—included the No Fly List, to identify those who should be prohibited from boarding flights, and the Selectee List, to identify those who should receive enhanced screening at airport checkpoints.

GAO was asked to assess the current status of the program. This report examines (1) changes to the Secure Flight program since 2009, (2) TSA's efforts to ensure that Secure Flight's screening determinations for passengers are implemented at airport checkpoints, and (3) the extent to which program performance measures assess progress toward goals. GAO analyzed TSA data and documents—including checkpoint data from 2012 through 2014 and Secure Flight performance measures—and interviewed relevant DHS officials.

What GAO Recommends

GAO recommends that TSA develop a process to regularly evaluate the root causes of screening errors at security checkpoints and implement measures to address these causes. GAO also recommends that TSA develop measures to address all aspects of performance related to program goals and develop a mechanism to systematically document the number and causes of Secure Flight system matching errors. DHS concurred with GAO's recommendations.

View GAO-14-531. For more information, contact Jennifer A. Grover at (202) 512-7141 or GroverJ@gao.gov.

What GAO Found

Since 2009, Secure Flight has changed from a program that identifies passengers as high risk solely by matching them against the No Fly and Selectee Lists to one that assigns passengers a risk category: high risk, low risk, or unknown risk. In 2010, following the December 2009 attempted attack of a U.S.-bound flight, which exposed gaps in how agencies used watchlists to screen individuals, the Transportation Security Administration (TSA) began using risk-based criteria to identify additional high-risk passengers who may not be in the Terrorist Screening Database (TSDB), but who should be designated as selectees for enhanced screening. Further, in 2011, TSA began screening against additional identities in the TSDB that are not already included on the No Fly or Selectee Lists. In addition, as part of TSA Pre✓™, a 2011 program through which TSA designates passengers as low risk for expedited screening, TSA began screening against several new lists of preapproved low-risk travelers. TSA also began conducting TSA Pre✓™ risk assessments, an activity distinct from matching against lists that uses the Secure Flight system to assign passengers scores based upon travel-related data, for the purpose of identifying them as low risk for a specific flight.

TSA has processes in place to implement Secure Flight screening determinations at airport checkpoints, but could take steps to enhance these processes. TSA information from May 2012 through February 2014 indicates that screening personnel have made errors in implementing Secure Flight determinations at the checkpoint. However, TSA does not have a process for systematically evaluating the root causes of these screening errors. GAO's interviews with TSA officials at airports yielded examples of root causes TSA could identify and address. Evaluating the root causes of screening errors, and then implementing corrective measures, in accordance with federal internal control standards, to address those causes could allow TSA to strengthen security screening at airports.

Since 2009, Secure Flight has established program goals that reflect new program functions to identify additional types of high-risk and also low-risk passengers; however, current program performance measures do not allow Secure Flight to fully assess its progress toward achieving all of its goals. For example, Secure Flight does not have measures to assess the extent of system matching errors. Establishing additional performance measures that adequately indicate progress toward goals would allow Secure Flight to more fully assess the extent to which it is meeting program goals. Furthermore, TSA lacks timely and reliable information on all known cases of Secure Flight system matching errors. More systematic documentation of the number and causes of these cases, in accordance with federal internal control standards, would help TSA ensure Secure Flight is functioning as intended.

This is a public version of a sensitive report that GAO issued in July 2014. Information that the Department of Homeland Security (DHS) and the Department of Justice deemed sensitive has been removed.

Contents

Figures

Abbreviations

ATS-P	Automated Targeting System-Passenger
BPSS	boarding pass scanning system
CAT	Credential Authentication Technology
CBP	U.S. Customs and Border Protection
CDC	Centers for Disease Control and Prevention
DHS	Department of Homeland Security
FBI	Federal Bureau of Investigation
GPRA	Government Performance and Results Act
IVCC	Identity Verification Call Center
OMB	Office of Management and Budget
OSO	Office of Security Operations
SFPD	Secure Flight Passenger Data
SOC	Secure Flight Operations Center
TDC	Travel Document Checker
TRIP	Traveler Redress Inquiry Program
TSA	Transportation Security Administration
TSBD	Terrorist Screening Database
TSO	Transportation Security Officer

September 9, 2014

The Honorable Michael T. McCaul
Chairman
The Honorable Bennie G. Thompson
Ranking Member
Committee on Homeland Security
House of Representatives

The Honorable Richard Hudson
Chairman
The Honorable Cedric L. Richmond
Ranking Member
Subcommittee on Transportation Security
Committee on Homeland Security
House of Representatives

The Honorable Mike Rogers
House of Representatives

The Transportation Security Administration's (TSA) Secure Flight program—established to identify those passengers who may pose security risks before boarding an aircraft—is a frontline defense against acts of terrorism that target the nation's civil aviation system. TSA developed and implemented Secure Flight in response to requirements in the Intelligence Reform and Terrorism Prevention Act of 2004 and a recommendation of the National Commission on Terrorist Attacks upon the United States (the 9/11 Commission) that TSA assume from air carriers the function of matching passengers against watchlists maintained by the federal government.[1] At the time, these watchlists, which were intended to identify high-risk individuals, included the No Fly List, composed of individuals who should be precluded from boarding an aircraft, and the Selectee List, composed of individuals who should

---

[1] See Pub. L. No. 108-458, § 4012(a), 118 Stat. 3638, 3714-18 (2004) (codified at 49 U.S.C. § 44903(j)(2)(C)). The 9/11 Commission, *The 9/11 Commission Report: Final Report of the National Commission on Terrorist Attacks upon the United States*, (Washington, D.C.: July 2004). TSA efforts to develop a computer-assisted passenger prescreening system predated the Intelligence Reform and Terrorism Prevention Act and the report of the 9/11 Commission.

receive enhanced screening at the airport security checkpoint.[2] After initiating the development of Secure Flight in August 2004, TSA began implementing the program in January 2009, and completed transitioning foreign and domestic air carriers to the program in November 2010. Secure Flight is now responsible for screening passengers and certain nontraveling individuals on all domestic and international commercial flights to, from, and within the United States; certain flights overflying the continental United States; and international point-to-point flights operated by U.S. aircraft operators.[3]

Beginning with a provision of the fiscal year 2004 Department of Homeland Security Appropriations Act and pursuant to requests by Congress, we have had regular and recurring responsibilities to assess and report on efforts by the Department of Homeland Security (DHS), of which TSA is a component, to develop and implement a passenger prescreening system, which TSA eventually implemented as Secure

---

[2]The No Fly and Selectee Lists are subsets of the Terrorist Screening Database (TSDB)—the U.S. government's consolidated watchlist of known or suspected terrorists. Not all identities within the TSDB are included on the No Fly and Selectee Lists; rather, to be included on either list, individuals must meet certain criteria specific to the list.

[3]In addition to passengers, Secure Flight screens certain nontraveling individuals, such as escorts for minor, elderly, and disabled passengers; airport and aircraft operator employees; and law enforcement officers who are authorized to access the airport's sterile area—the portion of an airport beyond the security screening checkpoint that provides passengers access to boarding aircraft and to which access is generally controlled through the screening of persons and property. See 49 C.F.R. § 1540.5. Also, Secure Flight began screening passengers on certain flights operated by foreign air carriers overflying United States airspace on October 24, 2012. Specifically, this includes flights over the continental United States, which includes the contiguous lower 48 states and excludes Hawaii and Alaska, and flights transiting the continental United States between two airports or locations in the same country where that country is Canada or Mexico. In addition, on October 31, 2013, Secure Flight began screening passengers traveling on certain Department of Defense flights. For purposes of this report, the terms "commercial flight" and "commercial aircraft operators" include the passenger operations of U.S. and foreign-flagged air carriers operating in accordance with 49 C.F.R. §§ 1544.101(a) and 1546.101(a)-(b), respectively. These terms correspond to "covered flight" and "covered aircraft operator," respectively as those terms are defined in the Secure Flight Final Rule. See 49 C.F.R. § 1560.3.

Flight.[4] In May 2009, we reported that after initial challenges, TSA had made significant strides in developing Secure Flight and that risks associated with implementing the program had been reduced.[5] Specifically, we reported on TSA's progress with respect to system accuracy, which involves activities to ensure that the Secure Flight system's automated matching of passenger and watchlist data correctly identifies passengers on watchlists. TSA designed the system to identify passengers who are the subject of watchlist records without producing an unacceptable number of misidentifications (incorrect matches). We reported in May 2009 that TSA was in the process of taking steps to test system accuracy, and without this testing, TSA would lack adequate assurance that Secure Flight would fully achieve its desired purpose and operate as intended. Therefore, to ensure the system was achieving its intended effects, we recommended that TSA periodically assess the accuracy of the Secure Flight system's matching capabilities and results. DHS concurred with our recommendation. In 2012, we reported that TSA responded to our recommendation by establishing a multidepartmental Match Review Board and its associated Match Review Board Working Group to, among other things, review performance measurement results and recommend changes to improve system performance.[6] Furthermore, TSA reported plans to periodically assess the extent to which the Secure Flight system did not identify individuals who are actual matches to the watchlist.[7]

---

[4]In 2003, TSA initiated work on developing a passenger prescreening system operated by the federal government. At the time, passenger prescreening involved U.S. and foreign air carriers matching passenger information against watchlists to identify passengers who should undergo additional security scrutiny. We performed this work in accordance with statutory mandates, beginning with the Department of Homeland Security Appropriations Act, 2004, Pub. L. No. 108-90, § 519, 117 Stat. 1137, 1155-56 (2003), and, most recently, the Department of Homeland Security Appropriations Act, 2009, Pub. L. No. 110-329, Div. D, § 512, 122 Stat. 3574, 3682-83 (2008), and pursuant to the requests of various congressional committees.

[5]GAO, *Aviation Security: TSA Has Completed Key Activities Associated with Implementing Secure Flight, but Additional Actions Are Needed to Mitigate Risks,* GAO-09-292 (Washington, D.C.: May 13, 2009).

[6]GAO, *Terrorist Watchlist: Routinely Assessing Impacts of Agency Actions since the December 25, 2009, Attempted Attack Could Help Inform Future Efforts,* GAO-12-476 (Washington, D.C.: May 31, 2012).

[7]GAO-12-476. These actions addressed our 2009 recommendation.

In May 2009, we also reported that passengers could attempt to provide fraudulent information when making an airline reservation to avoid Secure Flight detection.[8] For example, an individual on the No Fly or Selectee List could submit identifying information not included on the terrorist watchlist when making travel arrangements and, using a corresponding fraudulent identity document (such as a driver's license), pass through the security checkpoint undetected. At the time we issued our report, Secure Flight was aware of the vulnerability, but we did not assess any of the actions TSA was taking to address the problem because they were not part of our review.

In light of our prior work, you asked us to review the current status of the program, identify steps TSA has taken to address the Secure Flight vulnerability related to passengers providing fraudulent information, and report upon the effectiveness of TSA's efforts to assess Secure Flight system performance.

This report addresses the following questions:

1. How, if at all, has Secure Flight changed since implementation began in January 2009?

2. To what extent does TSA ensure that Secure Flight screening determinations for passengers are fully implemented at airport security checkpoints?

3. To what extent do TSA's performance measures appropriately assess progress toward achieving the Secure Flight program goals?

This report is a public version of the prior sensitive report that we provided to you. DHS and the Department of Justice deemed some of the information in the report as sensitive security information and law enforcement sensitive, respectively, both of which must be protected from public disclosure. Therefore, this report omits this sensitive information, which includes information about Secure Flight processes, high-risk lists used for screening, Secure Flight's ability to correctly identify individuals for screening, and the ability of Transportation Security Officers (TSO) to carry out Secure Flight determinations at the checkpoint. In some places throughout the report, we note that sensitive information was omitted from

---

[8]GAO-09-292.

the text in order to explain why additional details were not provided. Although the information provided in this report is more limited in scope, it addresses the same questions as the sensitive report. Also, the overall methodology used for both reports is the same.

To identify how the Secure Flight program has changed since 2009, we analyzed TSA documentation related to new agency initiatives involving Secure Flight screening, including the Secure Flight program concept of operations, privacy notices TSA issued from 2008 (in preparation for program implementation) through 2013, and TSA memorandums describing the rationale for new agency initiatives involving the Secure Flight system. We also submitted questions on changes to Secure Flight to TSA's Office of Chief Counsel and reviewed its written responses. To clarify our understanding of new agency initiatives to identify high- and low-risk passengers, we interviewed the officials responsible for implementing these initiatives from TSA and also U.S. Customs and Border Protection (CBP), which facilitates the generation of one high-risk list.

To determine the extent to which TSA ensures that the Secure Flight vetting results are fully implemented at airport security checkpoints, we analyzed TSA documents governing the screening checkpoint, such as standard operating procedures for checkpoint screening operations and Travel Document Checkers (TDC) and reviewed reports about the performance of TSOs at the checkpoint by TSA's Office of Inspections and GAO.[9] To determine the extent to which TSA made errors at the screening checkpoint, we analyzed certain TSA data on TSO performance at the screening checkpoint from May 2012, when TSA began tracking these data, through February 2014, when we conducted the analysis. We examined documentation about these data and interviewed knowledgeable officials, and determined that the data were sufficiently reliable for our purposes.[10] In addition, to clarify our understanding of TSA's checkpoint operations and inform our analysis, we interviewed officials with TSA's Office of Security Operations (OSO),

---

[9]For purposes of this report, and unless otherwise noted, references to TSOs, which include TDCs, include both TSA-employed screening personnel and screening personnel employed by a private sector company contracted with TSA to perform screening services at airports participating in TSA's Screening Partnership Program. See 49 U.S.C. § 44920.

[10]We did not evaluate the extent to which Secure Flight screening determinations for low-risk passengers are implemented at airport security checkpoints.

which is responsible for checkpoint operations, and officials at nine airports. We selected these nine airports based on a variety of factors, such as volume of passengers screened and geographic dispersion. The results of these interviews cannot be generalized to all airports, but provide insight into TSA's challenges to correctly identify and screen passengers at checkpoints. To better understand how TSA ensures that all passengers have been appropriately vetted by Secure Flight, we visited TSA's Identity Verification Call Center (IVCC) to interview officials and observe their identity verification procedures. We compared TSA's checkpoint procedures against *Standards for Internal Control in the Federal Government.*[11] Finally, to determine the extent to which TSA's planned technology solutions could address checkpoint errors, we analyzed documents, such as requests for proposals, related to TSA's planned technology solutions and interviewed knowledgeable TSA officials.

To determine the extent to which Secure Flight performance measures appropriately assess progress toward achieving the program's goals, we reviewed documentation of TSA's program goals and performance measures for fiscal years 2011 through 2013 and assessed these measures against provisions of the Government Performance and Results Act (GPRA) requiring agencies to compare actual results with performance goals.[12] We also interviewed relevant TSA officials about the fiscal year 2013 performance measures for the Secure Flight program and the adequacy of these measures in assessing TSA's progress in achieving program goals. In addition, to understand how TSA uses Secure Flight-related performance data, we reviewed documentation related to all meetings that TSA identified of the Secure Flight Match Review Board—a multidepartmental organization established to, among

---

[11]GAO, *Internal Control: Standards for Internal Control in the Federal Government*, GAO/AIMD-00-21.3.1 (Washington, D.C.: Nov. 1, 1999).

[12]See generally Government Performance and Results Act of 1993 (GPRA), Pub. L. No. 103-62, 107 Stat. 285 (1993). GPRA was updated by the GPRA Modernization Act of 2010, Pub. L. No. 111-352, 124 Stat. 3866 (2011). Although GPRA's requirements apply at the agency level, on the basis of our review of related GAO products, Office of Management and Budget (OMB) guidance, and studies by the National Academy of Public Administration and the Urban Institute, we have previously reported that these requirements can serve as leading practices in lower levels within an organization, such as with individual programs or initiatives. See GAO, *Pipeline Safety: Management of the Office of Pipeline Safety's Enforcement Program Needs Further Strengthening*, GAO-04-801 (Washington D.C.: Jul. 23, 2004).

other things, review performance measures and recommend changes to improve system performance—from the time the board was initiated, in March 2010, through August 2013, a total of 51 meetings. To identify the extent to which TSA monitors and evaluates the reasons for Secure Flight matching errors, we analyzed a list that TSA compiled at our request of missed passengers on two high-risk lists (including the reasons for these matching errors) that occurred from November 2010 through July 2013. We evaluated TSA's efforts to track cases in which TSA discovered a Secure Flight system matching error against *Standards for Internal Control in the Federal Government.*[13]

We conducted this performance audit from March 2013 to September 2014, in accordance with generally accepted government auditing standards. Those standards require that we plan and perform the audit to obtain sufficient, appropriate evidence to provide a reasonable basis for our findings and conclusions based on our audit objectives. We believe that the evidence obtained provides a reasonable basis for our findings and conclusions. Additional details on our scope and methodology are contained in appendix I.

Background

Responsibility for Secure Flight Operations

Several entities located within TSA's Office of Intelligence and Analysis share responsibility for administering the Secure Flight program. Among these are the Operations Strategy Mission Support Branch, which acts as the program's lead office; the Secure Flight Operations Branch, which oversees passenger vetting and other operational activities; and the Systems Management and Operations Branch and the Secure Flight Technology Branch, both of which focus on technology-related issues. Collectively, these entities received about $93 million to carry out program operations in fiscal year 2014.

---

[13]GAO/AIMD-00-21.3.1.

Overview of Secure Flight Matching and Screening Processes at Implementation

The Secure Flight program, as implemented pursuant to the 2008 Secure Flight Final Rule, requires U.S.- and foreign-based commercial aircraft operators traveling to, from, within, or overflying the United States, as well as U.S. commercial aircraft operators with international point-to-point flights, to collect information from passengers and transmit that information electronically to TSA.[14] This information, known collectively as Secure Flight Passenger Data (SFPD), includes personally identifiable information, such as full name, gender, date of birth, passport information (if available), and certain nonpersonally identifiable information, such as itinerary information and the unique number associated with a travel record (record number locator).[15]

Since implementation began in January 2009, the Secure Flight system has identified high-risk passengers by matching SFPD against the No Fly List and the Selectee List, subsets of the Terrorist Screening Database (TSDB), the U.S. government's consolidated watchlist of known or suspected terrorists maintained by the Terrorist Screening Center, a multiagency organization administered by the Federal Bureau of Investigation (FBI).[16] (We discuss screening activities initiated after TSA began implementing Secure Flight in 2009 later in this report.) To carry out this matching, the Secure Flight system conducts automated matching of passenger and watchlist data to identify a pool of passengers who are potential matches to the No Fly and Selectee Lists. Next, the system compares all potential matches against the TSA Cleared List, a list of individuals who have applied to, and been cleared through, the

---

[14]Secure Flight Program, 73 Fed. Reg. 64,018 (Oct. 28, 2008) (codified at 49 C.F.R. pt. 1560).

[15]See 49 C.F.R. § 1560.3. Aircraft operators must transmit available SFPD to Secure Flight approximately 72 hours prior to scheduled flight departure. For reservations created within 72 hours of flight departure, covered aircraft operators must submit passenger data as soon as they become available.

[16]Secure Flight also matches passenger data against the Centers for Disease Control and Prevention (CDC) Do Not Board List, which includes individuals who pose a significant health risk to other travelers and are not allowed to fly. The Do Not Board List is managed by CDC. See app. II for information on all the lists Secure Flight uses for screening.

DHS redress process.[17] Passengers included on the TSA Cleared List must submit a redress number when making a reservation, which allows the Secure Flight system to recognize and clear them.[18] After the system performs automated matching, Secure Flight analysts are to conduct manual reviews of potential matches, which may involve consulting other classified and unclassified data sources, to further rule out individuals who are not those included on the No Fly and Selectee Lists.

After the completion of manual reviews, TSA precludes passengers who remain potential matches to certain lists from receiving their boarding passes. These passengers, for whom air carriers receive a "passenger inhibited" message from Secure Flight, must undergo a resolution process at the airport. This process may involve air carriers sending updated passenger information back to Secure Flight for automated rematching or placing a call to Secure Flight for assistance in resolving the match.[19] At the conclusion of automated and manual screening processes (including the airport resolution process) air carriers may not issue a boarding pass to a passenger until they receive from Secure Flight a final screening determination. These determinations include a "cleared" message, for passengers found not to match a watchlist, and a "selectee" message, for matches to the Selectee List who are to be to be designated by air carriers for enhanced screening. For passengers matching the No Fly List, Secure Flight's initial "passenger inhibited" message is the final determination, and the air carrier may not issue a boarding pass (see fig. 1).

---

[17]The DHS Traveler Redress Inquiry Program (DHS TRIP) administers the TSA Cleared List. DHS established DHS TRIP in February 2007 to provide individuals, including those who believe they have been delayed or inconvenienced during travel because they have been wrongly identified as the subject of a watchlist record, an opportunity to be cleared. We have ongoing work on the extent to which DHS TRIP addresses delays and inconveniences associated with Secure Flight screening and expect to report on this work in September 2014.

[18]Because of the application of other TSA security measures, such as random selection, an individual's presence on the Cleared List will diminish, but not preclude, the possibility of being selected for enhanced screening. The technical term for redress number is "redress control number."

[19]This process may also involve the Secure Flight analyst contacting the Terrorist Screening Center for assistance in confirming or ruling out the match.

Figure 1: Secure Flight Screening as Implementation Began

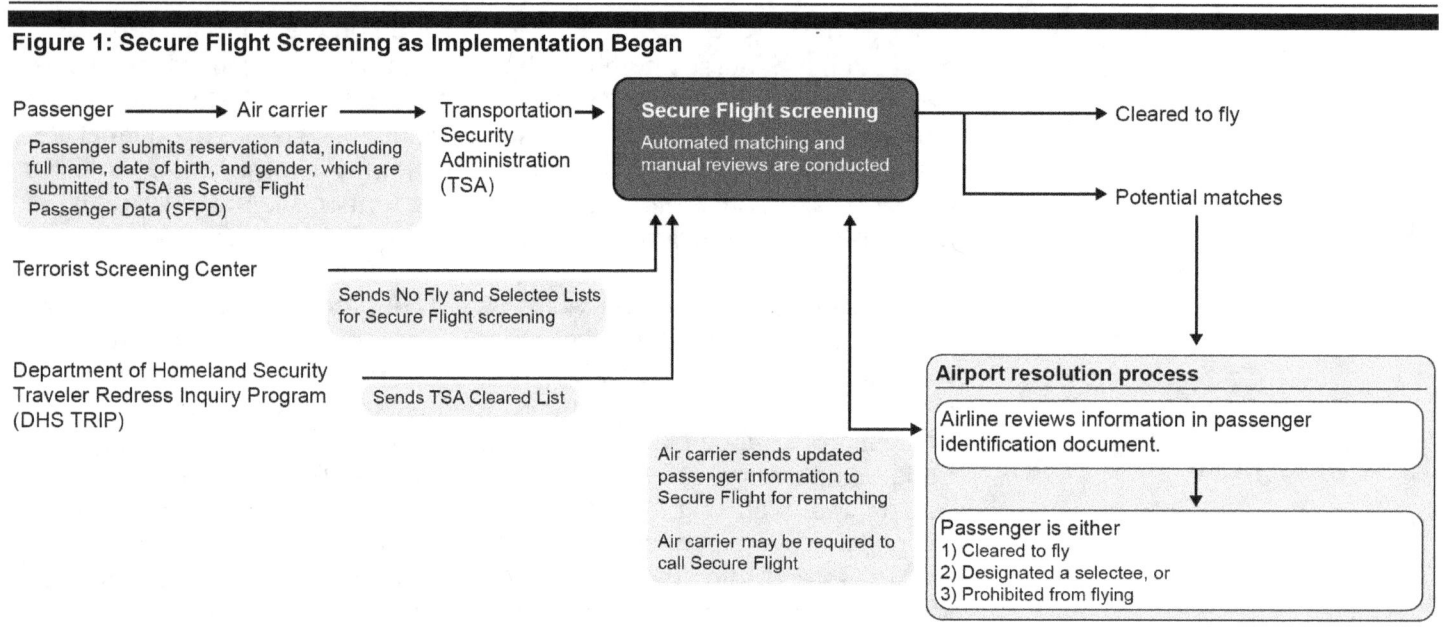

Source: GAO analysis of TSA information. | GAO-14-531

Passenger Screening at Airport Security Checkpoints

In general, passengers undergo one of three types of screening, based on the Secure Flight determinations shown on boarding passes—standard screening, enhanced screening for selectees, and expedited screening for low-risk passengers.[20] Standard screening typically includes a walk-through metal detector or Advanced Imaging Technology screening, which is to identify objects or anomalies concealed under clothing, and X-ray screening for the passenger's accessible property. In the event a walk-through metal detector triggers an alarm, the Advanced Imaging Technology identifies an anomaly, or the X-ray machine identifies a suspicious item, additional security measures, such as pat-downs, explosives trace detection searches (which involve a device certified by TSA to detect explosive particles), or additional physical searches may ensue as part of the resolution process. Enhanced screening includes, in addition to the procedures applied during a typical

---

[20]This section describes checkpoint screening activities as of May 2014. When Secure Flight implementation began, in 2009, TSA did not have a program in place to identify low-risk passengers eligible for expedited screening. We discuss more recent activities of TSA and the Secure Flight program to identify low-risk passengers for expedited screening later in this report.

standard screening experience, a pat-down and an explosives trace detection search or physical search of the interior of the passenger's accessible property, electronics, and footwear. Expedited screening typically includes walk-through metal detector screening and X-ray screening of the passenger's accessible property, but unlike in standard screening, travelers do not have to, among other things, remove their belts, shoes, or light outerwear. Passengers not designated for enhanced or expedited screening generally receive standard screening unless, for example, identified by TSA for a different type of screening through the application of random and unpredictable security measures at the screening checkpoint.[21]

Secure Flight Initially Identified Passengers on Terrorist Watchlists and Now Also Differentiates Passengers Based on Risk

Since January 2009, the Secure Flight program has changed from one that identifies high-risk passengers by matching them against the No Fly and Selectee Lists to one that assigns passengers a risk category: high risk, low risk, or unknown risk.[22] Specifically, Secure Flight now identifies passengers as high risk if they are matched to watchlists of known or suspected terrorists or other lists developed using certain high-risk criteria, as low risk if they are deemed eligible for expedited screening through TSA Pre✓™—a 2011 initiative to preapprove passengers for expedited screening—or through the application of low-risk rules, and as unknown risk if they do not fall within the other two risk categories. To separate passengers into these risk categories, TSA utilizes lists in addition to the No Fly and Selectee Lists, and TSA has adapted the Secure Flight system to perform risk assessments, a new system functionality that is distinct from both watchlist matching and matching against lists of known travelers. At airport checkpoints, those passengers identified as high risk receive enhanced screening, passengers identified

---

[21]Passengers who are to receive standard screening could receive expedited screening as part of Managed Inclusion at the screening checkpoint. Under Managed Inclusion, TSA randomly directs a certain percentage of passengers not otherwise designated that day as eligible for expedited screening to the expedited screening lane. Additionally, passengers designated for expedited screening may receive standard screening as part of random and unpredictable security measures. We expect to issue a report on expedited screening, including managed inclusion, later this year.

[22]The level of screening for a passenger may change from flight to flight based on the particulars of a flight or the individual.

as low risk are eligible for expedited screening, and passengers identified as unknown risk generally receive standard screening.[23]

Secure Flight Is Using New High-Risk Lists for Screening, Including Two Lists of Individuals Who Meet Various Threat Criteria, but Who May Not Be Known or Suspected Terrorists

Since January 2009, TSA has been using new high-risk lists for screening, including two lists to identify passengers who may not be known or suspected terrorists, but who—based on TSA's application of threat criteria—should receive enhanced screening, and an expanded list of known or suspected terrorists in the TSDB. As initially implemented under the October 2008 Secure Flight Final Rule, the program matched the names of passengers against the No Fly and Selectee List components of the TSDB. According to the rule, comparing passenger information against the No Fly and Selectee components of the TSDB (versus the entire TSDB) would be generally satisfactory during normal security circumstances to counter the security threat. The rule also provides that TSA may use the larger set of watchlists maintained by the federal government as warranted by security considerations, for example, if TSA learns that flights on a particular route may be subject to an increased security risk.[24] In such circumstances, TSA may decide to compare passenger information on some or all flights on that route against the full TSDB or other government databases, such as intelligence or law enforcement databases.

Rules-Based Watchlists

After the December 25, 2009, attempt to detonate a concealed explosive on board a U.S.-bound flight by an individual who was not a known or suspected terrorist in the TSDB, TSA sought to identify ways to mitigate unknown threats—individuals not in the TSDB for whom TSA has determined enhanced screening would be prudent. To that end, TSA worked with CBP to develop new lists for Secure Flight screening, and in April 2010, began using the lists to identify and designate for enhanced

[23]Passengers matched to the No Fly and CDC Do Not Board Lists are considered highest risk, and thus are not to receive boarding passes, and should not be allowed entry at airport checkpoints.

[24]Pursuant to the Intelligence Reform and Terrorism Prevention Act of 2004, TSA was to assume performance of the passenger prescreening function of comparing passenger information against the No Fly and Selectee Lists and utilize all appropriate records in the consolidated and integrated terrorist watchlist maintained by the federal government in performing that function. See 49 U.S.C. § 44903(j)(2)(C).

screening passengers who may represent unknown threats.[25] To create these lists, TSA leveraged CBP's access to additional data submitted by passengers traveling internationally and the capabilities of CBP's Automated Targeting System-Passenger (ATS-P)—a tool originally created and used by CBP that targets passengers arriving at or departing the United States by comparing their information against law enforcement, intelligence, and other enforcement data using risk-based targeting scenarios and assessments.[26] Specifically, analysts within the Intelligence and Analysis Division of TSA's Office of Intelligence and Analysis review current intelligence to identify factors that may indicate an elevated risk for a passenger. TSA creates rules based on these factors and provides them to CBP.[27] CBP then uses ATS-P to identify passengers who correspond with the rules and provides TSA information on them in the form of a list.[28] Upon receiving the list, TSA creates another rules-based list—a subset of the larger rules-based list—based on additional criteria. Through Secure Flight screening, TSA designates passengers matching either rules-based list as selectees for enhanced screening.[29]

---

[25]TSA uses two separate lists to address vulnerabilities exposed by the 2009 attempted attack. Further detail about these lists has been designated sensitive information, and thus cannot be included in a public report.

[26]CBP collects additional passenger information in order to fulfill its mission of securing the U.S. border while facilitating lawful travel and trade. See 19 C.F.R. § 122.49a(b)(3).

[27]These rules are criteria used by ATS-P to create the rules-based watchlists. The Department of Homeland Security's Office for Civil Rights and Civil Liberties, Privacy Office, and Office of the General Counsel are responsible for conducting quarterly reviews of these rules. The reviews are intended to ensure the rules are based on current intelligence identifying specific potential threats; are deactivated when no longer necessary to address those threats; are appropriately tailored to minimize the impact upon bona fide travelers' civil rights, civil liberties, and privacy; and are in compliance with relevant legal authorities, regulations, and DHS policies.

[28]According to TSA officials, individuals remain on the list for the time required to cover the scheduled travel.

[29]According to officials within TSA's Office of Chief Counsel, Secure Flight's use of rules-based watchlists is consistent with conducting watchlist matching under the "larger set of watchlists maintained by the Federal government as warranted by security considerations" as explained in the Secure Flight Final Rule, and nothing in statute or regulation prevents TSA from using non-TSDB-derived watchlists citing, among other provisions, 49 U.S.C. §§ 114 and 44903(j)(2)(C).

The Expanded Selectee List	In addition to the two ATS-P-generated lists, Secure Flight incorporated an additional list derived from the TSDB into its screening activities in order to designate more passengers who are known or suspected terrorists as selectees for enhanced screening.[30] Specifically, in April 2011, TSA began conducting watchlist matching against an Expanded Selectee List that includes all records in the TSDB with a full name (first name and surname) and full date of birth that meet the Terrorist Screening Center's reasonable suspicion standard to be considered a known or suspected terrorist, but that are not already included on the No Fly or Selectee List.[31] TSA began using the Expanded Selectee List in response to the December 25, 2009, attempted attack, as another measure to secure civil aviation. Collectively, the No Fly, Selectee, and Expanded Selectee Lists are used by Secure Flight to identify passengers from the government's consolidated database of known or suspected terrorists.[32]

---

[30]According to TSA officials, the entire TSDB is not used for Secure Flight screening because records with partial data (i.e., without first name, surname, and date of birth) could result in a significant increase in the number of passengers misidentified as being on the watchlist and cause unwarranted delay or inconvenience to travelers.

[31]All TSDB-based watchlists utilized by the Secure Flight program contain records determined to have met the reasonable suspicion standard. In general, to meet the reasonable suspicion standard, the agency nominating an individual for inclusion in the TSDB must consider the totality of information available that, taken together with rational inferences from that information, reasonably warrants a determination that an individual is known or suspected to be or have been knowingly engaged in conduct constituting, in preparation for, in aid of, or related to terrorism or terrorist activities. As previously discussed, to be included on the No Fly and Selectee Lists, individuals must meet criteria specific to these lists. The TSDB, which is the U.S. government's consolidated watchlist of known or suspected terrorists, also contains records on additional populations of individuals that do not meet the reasonable suspicion standard articulated above that other federal agencies utilize to support their border and immigration screening missions.

[32]Secure Flight also randomly identifies passengers as selectees for enhanced screening.

Secure Flight Is Identifying Low-Risk Passengers by Screening against TSA Pre✓™ Lists and Conducting Passenger Risk Assessments

Since October 2011, TSA has also begun using Secure Flight to identify passengers as low risk, and therefore eligible for expedited screening, through the use of new screening lists and by performing passenger risk assessments.[33] According to TSA, identifying more passengers as eligible for expedited screening will permit TSA to reduce screening resources for low-risk travelers, thereby enabling TSA to concentrate screening resources on higher-risk passenger populations. In August 2013, TSA officials stated that this approach would support the agency's goal of identifying 25 percent of airline passengers as eligible for expedited screening by the end of calendar year 2013. As of May 2014, TSA officials stated the goal had been revised to identify 50 percent of airline passengers as eligible for expedited screening by the end of calendar year 2014.[34] According to officials within TSA's Office of Chief Counsel, TSA's efforts to identify low-risk travelers also fulfill a stated goal of the 2008 Secure Flight rule to implement a "known traveler" concept that would allow the federal government to assign a unique number to known travelers for whom the federal government had conducted a threat assessment and determined did not pose a security threat.

TSA Pre✓™ Lists of Preapproved Low-Risk Travelers

In 2011, TSA's Office of Risk-Based Security began implementing TSA Pre✓™, a program that allows TSA to differentiate passengers into a low-risk screening category and therefore identify them as eligible for expedited screening.[35] As part of TSA's effort to implement the TSA Pre✓™ program, Secure Flight has begun screening against several new lists of preapproved, low-risk travelers to identify passengers who are eligible for expedited screening.[36] In October 2011, Secure Flight began screening against the first of these lists, which contained information on certain members of three CBP trusted traveler programs (programs in which applicants submit to federal background checks to be approved as low-risk travelers eligible to receive expedited processing at ports of

---

[33]When TSA, through Secure Flight, determines that a passenger is eligible for expedited screening, the passenger's boarding pass is encoded so that he or she is routed to the proper screening lane.

[34]TSA also tracks the number of passengers who receive expedited screening.

[35]We expect to issue a report on TSA's Pre✓™ program later this year.

[36]Individuals on the TSA Pre✓™ lists receive Known Traveler Numbers that they must submit when making travel reservations to be identified as low-risk. See 49 C.F.R. § 1560.3 (defining "Known Traveler Number"). TSA also refers to these lists as Known Traveler lists.

entry).[37] Since then, TSA has established separate TSA Pre✓™ lists for additional low-risk passenger populations, including members of the U.S. armed forces, Congressional Medal of Honor Society members, and members of the Homeland Security Advisory Council (see app. II for a full listing of TSA Pre✓™ lists used by Secure Flight for screening).[38] To identify these and other low-risk populations, TSA coordinated and entered into agreements with a lead agency or outside entity willing to compile and maintain the associated TSA Pre✓™ list.[39] Members of the list-based, low-risk populations participating in TSA Pre✓™ are provided a unique known traveler number, and their personal identifying information (name and date of birth), along with the known traveler number, is included on lists used by Secure Flight for screening.

In addition to TSA Pre✓™ lists sponsored by other agencies or entities, TSA created its own TSA Pre✓™ list composed of individuals who apply to be preapproved as low-risk travelers through the TSA Pre✓™ Application Program, an initiative launched in December 2013.[40] The program is another DHS trusted traveler program, in which DHS collects a fee to conduct a background investigation for applicants.[41] Applicants approved as low risk through the program receive a known traveler number and are included on an associated TSA Pre✓™ Application Program list used by Secure Flight for screening. To be recognized as

---

[37]The three CBP Trusted Traveler programs are NEXUS, SENTRI, and Global Entry. See GAO, *Trusted Travelers: Programs Provide Benefits but Enrollment Processes Could Be Strengthened*, GAO-14-483 (Washington, D.C.: May 30, 2014).

[38]As of March 2014, the TSA Pre✓™ list for the U.S. armed forces included eligible members of the Army, Navy, Marine Corps, Air Force, and Coast Guard.

[39]According to TSA officials, per these agreements, agencies are to maintain the lists by ensuring that individuals continue to meet the criteria for inclusion and to update the lists as needed. We did not review the extent to which agencies are maintaining the lists.

[40]TSA leveraged existing federal capabilities to both enroll and conduct background checks for program applicants. For example, for the TSA Pre✓™ Application Program, TSA is using enrollment centers previously established for the Transportation Worker Identification Credential Program (TSA's program to provide a biometric credential to certain transportation workers) and existing transportation vetting systems to conduct applicant background checks.

[41]An applicant must be a U.S. citizen, U.S. national, or lawful permanent resident and cannot have been convicted of certain crimes. To apply, individuals must visit an enrollment center, provide biographic information (name, date of birth, and address) and valid identity and citizenship documentation, and be fingerprinted. The program requires a nonrefundable application processing fee of $85.00.

low risk by the Secure Flight system, individuals on TSA Pre✓™ lists must submit their known traveler numbers when making a flight reservation.[42] As of April 2014, there were about 5.6 million individuals who, through TSA Pre✓™ program lists, were eligible for expedited screening.[43]

TSA Pre✓™ Risk Assessments

To further increase the number of passengers identified as low risk (and therefore TSA Pre✓™ eligible), TSA adapted the Secure Flight system to begin assigning passengers risk scores to designate them as low risk for a specific flight. Beginning in 2011, TSA piloted a risk-based security program to identify certain members of participating airlines' frequent flier programs as low risk, and therefore eligible for expedited screening for a specific flight.[44] Specifically, TSA used the Secure Flight system to assess data submitted by these frequent fliers during the course of travel and assign them scores, which were then used to determine eligibility for expedited screening. In October 2013, TSA expanded the use of these assessments to all passengers, not just frequent fliers, and also began using other travel-related data to assess passengers.[45] These assessments are conducted only if the passenger has not been designated as high risk by other Secure Flight screening activities or matched to one of the TSA Pre✓™ Lists. The scores assigned to passengers correspond with a certain likelihood of being designated as eligible to receive expedited screening through TSA Pre✓™.[46] According

---

[42]Passengers identified by Secure Flight as low risk are eligible for expedited screening through TSA Pre✓™, but may not receive this expedited screening. For example, TSA Pre✓™ includes a level of randomness to ensure unpredictable results. One potential result of the randomness is that a passenger who is eligible to receive expedited screening may instead be randomly selected to receive standard or enhanced screening.

[43]In July 2012, TSA also began screening against a TSA Pre✓™ Disqualification Protocol List, a watchlist created and maintained by TSA that includes individuals who, based upon their involvement in violations of security regulations of sufficient severity or frequency (e.g., bringing a loaded firearm to the checkpoint), are disqualified from receiving expedited screening for some period of time or permanently.

[44]Only those frequent flier members who meet the criteria established by TSA are eligible for these assessments. Because Secure Flight does not collect or maintain frequent flier information, air carriers signal to TSA which passengers meet these criteria.

[45]In addition, TSA continues to use frequent flier data to identify as low risk those individuals who opted into the TSA Pre✓™ program through their airline during the pilot.

[46]Also, because these TSA Pre✓™ risk assessments identify percentages of passengers likely to have received expedited screening, the same passenger who is TSA Pre✓™ eligible on one flight may not be designated as such on another flight.

to officials within TSA's Office of Chief Counsel, the assessments are not watchlist matching, rather they are a means to facilitate the secure travel of the public—a purpose of Secure Flight, as stated in the program's final rule and in accordance with TSA's statutory responsibilities to ensure the security of civil aviation.

As of May 2014, TSA uses Pre✓™ risk assessments to determine a passenger's low-risk status and resulting eligibility for TSA Pre✓™ expedited screening, but according to TSA officials, TSA also has the capability to use this functionality to identify high-risk passengers for enhanced screening. TSA made adjustments to enable the Secure Flight system to perform TSA Pre✓™ risk assessments to identify high-risk passengers in March 2013. However, TSA officials stated the agency has no immediate plans to use the assessments to identify high-risk passengers beyond those already included on watchlists.

New Secure Flight Screening Activities Allow TSA to Differentiate Passengers by Risk Category

Given the changes in the program since implementation, the current Secure Flight system screens passengers and returns one of four screening results to the air carriers for each passenger: TSA Pre✓™ eligible (expedited screening), cleared to fly (standard screening), selectee (enhanced screening), or do not board (see fig. 2).

Figure 2: Secure Flight Screening to Identify High- and Low-Risk Passengers

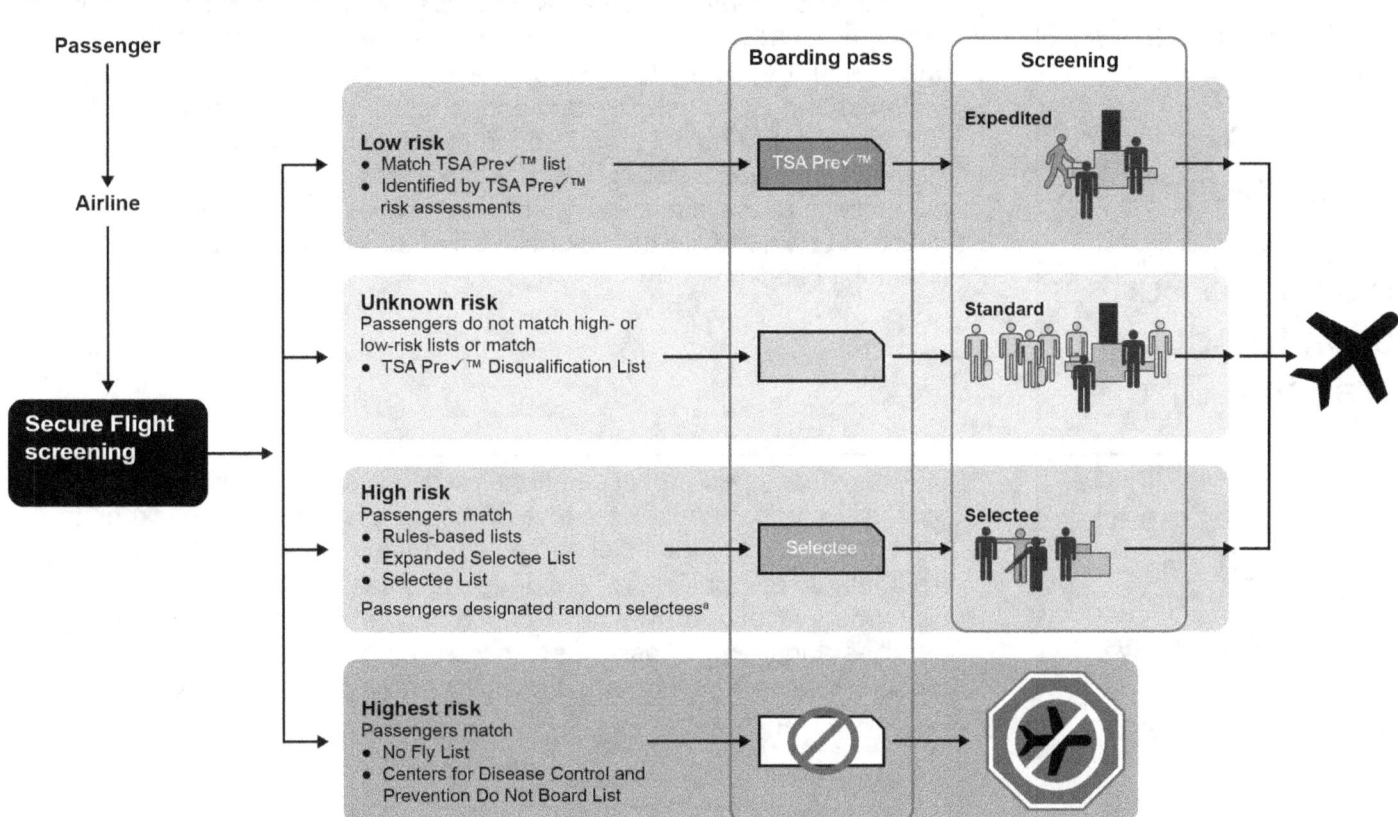

Source: GAO analysis of TSA information. | GAO-14-531

[a]These passengers are identified for enhanced screening at random; they not are included on government watchlists.

TSA Has Processes in Place to Implement Secure Flight Screening Determinations at Checkpoints, but Could Take Further Action to Address Screening Errors

TSA has developed processes to help ensure that individuals and their accessible property receive a level of screening at airport checkpoints that corresponds to the level of risk determined by Secure Flight.[47] However, TSA could take additional actions to prevent TSO errors in implementing these risk determinations at the screening checkpoint. Furthermore, fraudulent identification or boarding passes could enable individuals to evade Secure Flight vetting, creating a potential vulnerability at the screening checkpoint. TSA's planned technology solutions could reduce the risk posed by fraudulent documents at the screening checkpoint.

TSA Has Developed Processes to Implement Secure Flight Determinations at Airport Checkpoints

TSA has developed processes to help ensure that individuals and their accessible property receive a level of screening at airport checkpoints that corresponds to the level of risk determined by Secure Flight.[48] TDCs are primarily responsible for ensuring that passengers receive the appropriate level of screening because they are to verify passengers' identities and identify passengers' screening designations. TSA requires passengers to present photo identification and a boarding pass at the

---

[47]At airports participating in TSA's Screening Partnership Program, private companies under contract to TSA are to perform screening functions with TSA supervision and in accordance with TSA standard operating procedures. See 49 U.S.C. § 44920. At these airports, private sector screeners, and not TSA employees, have responsibility for screening passengers and their property. For purposes of this report, references to TSOs include both TSA employees and screeners employed by private screening contractors.

[48]This report focuses on TSA efforts to ensure that individuals receive appropriate levels of screening at U.S. airports. At foreign airports, U.S.- and foreign-flagged air carrier operations destined for the United States are responsible for ensuring that passengers and their carry-on baggage are screened according to their risk level—consistent with requirements in the air carriers' TSA-approved security programs and any applicable TSA security directives or emergency amendments. See generally 49 C.F.R. pts. 1544 and 1546. Unlike at U.S. airports, TSA does not conduct or oversee screening operations at foreign airports. Therefore, we are not discussing passenger screening at foreign airports in this report. TSA's Office of Global Strategies inspects air carrier compliance with Secure Flight-related requirements at foreign airports. We reported in October 2011 on the challenges the Office of Global Strategies faces in this process, including limited access to some foreign airports. See GAO, *Aviation Security: TSA Has Taken Steps to Enhance Its Foreign Airport Assessments, but Opportunities Exist to Strengthen the Program,* GAO-12-163 (Washington, D.C.: Oct. 21, 2011).

screening checkpoint.[49] Using lights and magnifiers, which allow the TDC to examine security features on the passenger's identification documents, the TDC is to examine the identification and boarding pass to confirm that they appear genuine and pertain to the passenger. The TDC is also to confirm that the data included on the boarding pass and in the identity document match one another. According to TSA standard operating procedures, TDCs may accept minor name variations between the passenger's boarding pass and identification.[50] If the TDC finds that the information on the identification varies significantly from the boarding pass, the TDC is to refer the passenger to another TSA representative for identity verification through TSA's Identity Verification Call Center (IVCC). If the passenger's information varies from the SFPD submitted to Secure Flight, the IVCC is to contact Secure Flight to vet the new information. If the identification or boarding pass appears fraudulent, the TDC is to contact law enforcement.

The TDC is also required to review the passenger's boarding pass to identify his or her Secure Flight passenger screening determination—that is, whether the passenger should receive standard, enhanced, or expedited screening. TDCs either examine the boarding pass manually or, where available, scan the boarding pass using an electronic boarding pass scanning system (BPSS). In addition, Secure Flight provides TSA officials in the airports with advance notice of upcoming selectees from the Selectee and Expanded Selectee Lists, as well as those on the No Fly List. Secure Flight provides this information to TSA officials at the passenger's airport of departure via e-mail beginning 72 hours prior to flight departure for the No Fly and Selectee Lists, and via a shared electronic posting beginning 26 to 29 hours prior to flight departure for the Expanded Selectee List.

TSA also has requirements related to TDC performance. First, according to TSA officials, TSA designated the TDC a qualified position in February 2013, meaning that TSOs must complete training and pass a job knowledge test to qualify as TDCs. Second, TSA has documented processes to govern the screening checkpoint, such as standard

---

[49]In November 2007, in addition to allowing paper boarding passes, TSA began allowing air carriers to issue mobile boarding passes, which, for example, passengers may download to their cell phones.

[50]These variations are identified in the TDC standard operating procedures.

operating procedures applicable to the TDC, the screening checkpoint, and expedited screening that specify responsibilities and lines of reporting. In March 2011, TSA also updated its Screening Management standard operating procedures to clarify that supervisory TSOs are required to monitor TSO performance to ensure compliance with all applicable standard operating procedures and correct improper or faulty application of screening procedures to ensure effective, vigilant, and courteous screening. According to officials in TSA's Office of Inspection, many checkpoint failures resulted from a lack of supervision. These officials stated that when TDCs are not properly supervised, they are more likely to take shortcuts and miss steps in the standard operating procedures and that because working as a TDC can be tedious and repetitive, supervision and regular rotation are particularly important to ensure TDCs' continued vigilance.

TSOs Have Made Errors in Implementing Secure Flight Screening Determinations at the Screening Checkpoint, and Additional Actions Could Reduce the Number of Screening Errors

Our analysis of TSA information from May 2012 through February 2014 found that TSOs have made errors in implementing Secure Flight risk determinations at the screening checkpoint.[51] By evaluating the root causes of these errors and implementing corrective measures to address those root causes, TSA could reduce the risk posed by TSO error at the screening checkpoint. TSA officials we spoke with at five of the nine airports conduct after-action reviews of screening errors at the checkpoint and have used these reviews to take action to address the root causes of those errors. However, TSA does not have a systematic process for evaluating the root causes of screening errors at the checkpoint across airports, which could allow TSA to identify trends across airports and target nationwide efforts to address these issues.

TSA OSO officials told us that evaluating the root causes of screening errors would be helpful and could allow them to better target TSO training efforts. In January 2014, TSA OSO officials stated that they are in the early stages of forming a group to discuss these errors. However, TSA was not able to provide documentation of the group's membership, purpose, goals, time frames, or methodology. *Standards for Internal Control in the Federal Government* states that managers should compare actual performance with expected results and analyze significant

---

[51]The details of these screening errors are considered sensitive information.

differences.[52] As TSA moves forward with its plans to form this group, it will be important for TSA to develop a process for evaluating the root causes of screening errors at the checkpoint and identify and implement corrective measures, as needed, to address these root causes. Uncovering and addressing the root causes of screening errors could help TSA reduce the number of these errors at the checkpoint.

Fraudulent Documents Pose Risks at Airport Screening Checkpoints, and TSA's Planned Technology Solutions Are in Early Stages

Fraudulent identification or boarding passes could enable individuals to evade Secure Flight vetting, creating a potential vulnerability at the screening checkpoint. TDCs are responsible for verifying the validity of identification documents and boarding passes presented by passengers. In June 2012, the TSA Assistant Administrator for the Office of Security Capabilities testified before Congress that the wide variety of identifications and boarding passes presented to TDCs poses challenges to effective manual verification of passenger identity, ticketing, and vetting status.[53] He testified that there are at least 2,470 different variations of identification that could be presented at security checkpoints and stated that it is very difficult for a TSO to have a high level of proficiency for all of those identifications. From May 2012 through July 2013, TSA denied 1,384 individuals access to the sterile area as a result of identity checking procedures. These denials include travelers who did not appear to match the photo on their identification, who presented identification that appeared fraudulent or showed signs of tampering, and who were unwilling or unable to provide identifying information.[54] During this same time period, TDCs also made 852 referrals to airport law enforcement because of travelers who did not appear to match the photo on their identification, presented identification or boarding passes that appeared fraudulent or showed signs of tampering, or exhibited suspicious behaviors. However, TSA would not know how many travelers successfully flew with fraudulent documents unless those individuals came to TSA's attention for another reason.

---

[52]GAO/AIMD-00-21.3.1.

[53]Statement of Kelly Hoggan, Assistant Administrator, TSA Office of Security Capabilities, before the House Committee on Homeland Security, Subcommittee on Transportation Security, June 19, 2012.

[54]See, e.g., 49 C.F.R. § 1540.107(c) (prohibiting, in general, an individual from entering a sterile area or boarding an aircraft if the individual does not present a verifying identity document when requested for purposes of watchlist matching).

We have previously reported on security vulnerabilities involving the identity verification process at the screening checkpoint. For example, in our May 2009 report on Secure Flight, we identified a vulnerability involving the Secure Flight system—namely, airline passengers could provide fraudulent information when making a flight reservation to avoid detection.[55] In addition, in June 2012, we reported on several instances when passengers used fraudulent documentation to board flights. For example, we reported that in 2006, a university student created a website that enabled individuals to create fake boarding passes. In addition, in 2011, a man was convicted of stowing away aboard an aircraft after using an expired boarding pass with someone else's name on it to fly from New York to Los Angeles. We also reported that news reports have highlighted the apparent ease of ordering high-quality counterfeit driver's licenses from China.[56]

TSA's planned technology solutions could reduce the risk posed by fraudulent documents at the screening checkpoint. Boarding pass scanners are designed to verify the digital signature on these boarding passes, allowing TDCs to know that the boarding passes are genuine. The scanners are also to notify the TDC when a passenger is a selectee.[57] In September 2013, TSA purchased 1,400 boarding pass scanners, at a cost of $2.6 million, and planned to deploy 1 for every TDC at airport security checkpoints, beginning with TDCs in TSA Pre✓™ lines. According to TSA officials, as of March 2014, TSA had deployed all 1,400 scanners at airport security checkpoints.[58]

In December 2013, TSA released a request for proposal for Credential Authentication Technology (CAT), which is a system that is designed to verify passenger identity, ticketing status, and Secure Flight risk

---

[55]GAO-09-292.

[56]GAO, *Aviation Security: Status of TSA's Acquisition of Technology for Screening Passenger Identification and Boarding Passes*, GAO-12-826T (Washington, D.C.: June 19, 2012).

[57]Boarding pass scanners also indicate when a passenger is eligible for expedited screening through TSA Pre✓™.

[58]TSA initially used boarding pass scanners provided and owned by airlines to scan TSA Pre✓™ and mobile boarding passes. According to TSA officials, as these airline-owned scanners become inoperable, TSA plans to phase them out and replace them with TSA-owned scanners.

determination at the screening checkpoint. CAT could address the risks of fraudulent identifications, as well as TSO error and reliance on air carriers to properly issue boarding passes. CAT is to verify the authenticity of identification documents presented at the screening checkpoint, confirm the passenger's reservation, and provide the Secure Flight screening result for that traveler. TDCs would no longer need to examine passengers' boarding passes to identify those who should receive enhanced screening, which could reduce the potential for error. In April 2014, TSA awarded a contract for the CAT technology solution.

TSA has faced long-standing challenges in acquiring CAT technology. In May 2009, we found that TSA had begun working to address the vulnerability posed by airline passengers providing fraudulent information when making a flight reservation to avoid detection. TSA has issued four previous requests for proposals for CAT/BPSS technology, two of which resulted in no vendors meeting minimum requirements. In 2012, TSA piloted a joint CAT/BPSS technology from three vendors at a cost of $4.4 million. According to TSA's final report on the pilot, TSA decided not to move forward with these systems because of significant operability and performance difficulties. None of the units tested met TSA's throughput requirements, creating delays at the screening checkpoint. According to TSA officials, after the joint CAT/BPSS pilot failed, TSA decided to separate CAT technology from BPSS technology and procure each separately.

TSA has also faced challenges in estimating the costs associated with the CAT system. In June 2012, we reported that we could not evaluate the credibility of TSA's life-cycle cost estimate for CAT/BPSS because it did not include an independent cost estimate or an assessment of how changing key assumptions and other factors would affect the estimate.[59] At that time, according to the life-cycle cost estimate for the Passenger Screening Program, of which CAT/BPSS is a part, the estimated 20-year life-cycle cost of CAT/BPSS was approximately $130 million based on a procurement of 4,000 units. As of April 2014, TSA had not approved a new life-cycle cost estimate for the CAT program, so we were unable to evaluate the extent to which TSA has addressed these challenges in its new estimate.

---

[59]GAO-12-826T.

TSA Lacks Key Information to Determine whether the Secure Flight Program Is Achieving Its Goals

Secure Flight Measures Do Not Fully Assess Progress toward Goals

Secure Flight has six program goals that are relevant to the results of screening performed by the Secure Flight computer system and the program analysts who review computer-generated matches, including the following:

- goal 1: prevent individuals on the No Fly List from boarding an aircraft,

- goal 2: identify individuals on the Selectee List for enhanced screening,

- goal 3: support TSA's risk-based security mission by identifying high-risk passengers for appropriate security measures/actions and identifying low-risk passengers for expedited screening,

- goal 4: minimize misidentification of individuals as potential threats to aviation security,

- goal 5: incorporate additional risk-based security capabilities to streamline processes and accommodate additional aviation populations, and

- goal 6: protect passengers' personal information from unauthorized use and disclosure.

To assess progress with respect to these goals, the program has nine performance measures that it reports on externally (see app. III for the nine Secure Flight performance measures and performance results for fiscal years 2012 and 2013).[60] In addition, Secure Flight has measures for a number of other program activities that it reports internally to program managers to keep them apprised of program performance with respect to the goals (such as the number of confirmed matches identified to the No Fly and Selectee Lists).[61]

However, Secure Flight's performance measures do not fully assess progress toward achieving its six program goals. For goals 1 through 4 and goal 6, we found that while TSA measured some aspects of performance related to these goals, it did not measure aspects of performance necessary to determine overall progress toward the goals. In addition, for goal 5, we could not identify any program measures that represented the type of performance required to make progress toward achieving the goal, in part because the goal itself did not specify how performance toward the goal should be measured. GPRA establishes a framework for strategic planning and performance measurement in the federal government.[62] Part of that framework involves agencies establishing quantifiable performance measures to demonstrate how they intend to achieve their program goals and measure the extent to which they have done so. These measures should adequately indicate progress toward performance goals so that agencies can compare their programs' actual results with desired results.[63] Our prior body of work has shown

---

[60]Secure Flight program management reports externally (to DHS and the Office of Management and Budget (OMB)) on nine measures. Specifically, Secure Flight reports to DHS on six Key Performance Parameters, which are key system capabilities that must be met for a system to meet its operational goals. In addition, Secure Flight reports on five measures to OMB as part of its yearly exhibit 300, also called the Capital Asset Plan and Business Case—a document that agencies submit to OMB to justify resource requests for major information technology (IT) investments. Two of the Key Performance Parameters and OMB measures are the same; therefore, the program reports externally on nine distinct measures.

[61]The measures are contained on the Secure Flight Executive Dashboard, a compilation of data capturing various aspects of Secure Flight's operations on a weekly, monthly, and year-to-date basis.

[62]Government Performance and Results Act of 1993, Pub. L. No. 103-62, 107 Stat. 285 (1993). GPRA was updated by the GPRA Modernization Act of 2010. Pub. L. No. 111-352, 124 stat. 3866 (2011).

[63]GAO, *Agencies' Annual Performance Plans under the Results Act: An Assessment Guide to Facilitate Congressional Decisionmaking,* GAO/GGD/AIMD,10.1.18 (Washington, D.C.: February 1998), and *The Results Act: An Evaluator's Guide to Assessing Agency Annual Performance Plans,* GAO/GGD-10.1.20 (Washington, D.C.: April 1998).

that measures adequately indicate progress toward performance goals when they represent the important dimensions of their performance goals and reflect the core functions of their related programs or activities.[64] Further, when performance goals are not self-measuring, performance measures should translate those goals into concrete conditions that determine what data to collect in order to learn whether the program has made progress in achieving its goal.[65]

Measures Addressing Accuracy (Goals 1 through 4)

With respect to the program's first four goals, which address the Secure Flight system's ability to accurately identify passengers on various watchlists for high- and low-risk screening, the program does not measure all aspects of performance that are essential to achieving these goals. To measure performance toward the first three goals, Secure Flight collects various types of data, including the number of passengers TSA identifies as matches to high- and low-risk lists (including the No Fly, Selectee, Expanded Selectee, rules-based, and TSA Pre✓™ lists). However, Secure Flight has no measures to address the extent to which Secure Flight is missing passengers who are actual matches to these lists (see table 1).

[64]GAO/GGD-10.1.20.

[65]GAO/GGD-10.1.20.

Table 1: Key Aspects of Secure Flight Performance, with Respect to Accuracy-Related Program Goals, Including Performance That Is Not Being Measured

Goals	Secure Flight performance measures that address goal	Performance that TSA does not measure
1. Prevent individuals on the No Fly List from boarding an aircraft	• **Potential matches:** TSA collects and regularly reviews data on the number of passengers identified as a potential matches to the No Fly List by the Secure Flight system. • **Confirmed matches:** TSA collects and regularly reviews data on the number of passengers confirmed as being individuals on the No Fly List.	• **Missed No Flys:** Passengers on the No Fly List who were not identified as matches by the Secure Flight system.
2. Identify individuals on the Selectee List for enhanced screening	• **Potential matches:** TSA collects and regularly reviews data on the number of passengers identified as potential matches to the Selectee List by the Secure Flight system. • **Confirmed matches:** TSA collects and regularly reviews data on the number of passengers confirmed as being individuals on the Selectee List.	• **Missed selectees:** Passengers on the Selectee List who were not identified as matches by the Secure Flight system.
3. Support TSA's Risk-Based Security mission by identifying high- and low-risk passengers for appropriate screening	• **Potential matches to high-risk lists:** In addition to regularly reviewing data on potential matches to the No Fly and Selectee Lists (see 1 and 2 above), TSA collects and regularly reviews data on the number of passengers identified by the Secure Flight system as potential matches to the Expanded Selectee and rules-based lists. • **Passengers identified as low risk:** TSA collects and regularly reviews data on the number of boarding passes identified as TSA Pre✓™ eligible by the Secure Flight system—including passengers matched to TSA Pre✓™ lists and those identified through Pre✓™ risk assessments.	• **Missed high-risk passengers:** Passengers on any high-risk list (No Fly, Selectee, Expanded Selectee, or rules-based) who were not identified as matches by the Secure Flight system. • **Missed low-risk passengers:** Passengers on TSA Pre✓™ Lists who were not identified as matches by the Secure Flight system.
4. Minimize misidentification of individuals as potential threats to aviation security	• **Misidentifications:** TSA collects and regularly reviews data on its rate of false positives—the percentage of passengers who, upon arrival at the airport, are found to be incorrectly identified as matches to the No Fly and Selectee Lists—and on the number of passengers cleared through the TSA Cleared List.	• **Misidentifications to all high-risk lists:** Secure Flight's performance measure does not account for the number of passengers incorrectly identified as being on the Expanded Selectee or rules-based lists.

Source: GAO analysis of Transportation Security Administration (TSA) data. | GAO-14-531

TSA Secure Flight officials stated that measuring the extent to which the Secure Flight system may miss passengers on high-risk lists is difficult to perform in real time.[66] However, our prior work and current program documentation show that the Secure Flight program has used proxy methods to assess the extent to which the system is missing passengers on watchlists. For example, we reported in May 2009 that when the Secure Flight system was under development, TSA conducted a series of tests—using a simulated passenger list and a simulated watchlist created by a TSA contractor with expertise in watchlist matching—to measure the extent to which Secure Flight did not identify all simulated watchlist records.[67] In addition, for this review, we examined meeting minutes of the Secure Flight Match Review Board—a multidepartmental board that reviews system performance and recommends changes—for the period May 2010 through August 2013, to determine how the board assesses system performance. The minutes show that Secure Flight, when contemplating a change in the system's search capabilities, measures the impacts of proposed changes on system performance, including the extent to which the changes result in failures to identify watchlisted individuals. To make these assessments, Secure Flight rematches historical passenger data and watchlist data under proposed system changes, and compares the results with prior Secure Flight screening outcomes to determine whether any previously identified individuals on high-risk lists were missed.[68] While helpful for Match Review Board deliberations, the testing reflected in meeting minutes was performed on an ad hoc basis and therefore is not a substitute for ongoing performance measurement.

In addition, with respect to low-risk lists, TSA could measure the extent to which the Secure Flight system correctly identifies passengers submitting valid known traveler numbers (i.e., an actual number on a TSA Pre✓™

---

[66]Further details on the challenges TSA faces in identifying when Secure Flight may miss individuals on lists is sensitive information and therefore could not be included in a public report.

[67]GAO-09-292.

[68]These passenger data are available to Secure Flight for testing purposes because the system retains passenger data and the results of Secure Flight matches in the system for up to 7 days after completion of the passenger's directional travel. After 7 days, all data for passengers not identified as matches to a high-risk watchlist must be expunged from the system.

list) and designates them for expedited screening.[69] TSA officials have stated that variations in the way passengers enter information when making a reservation with a valid known traveler number can cause the system to fail to identify them as TSA Pre✓™ eligible. For example, TSA Match Review Board documentation from December 2012 identified that the Secure Flight system had failed to identify participants on one TSA Pre✓™ list because they used honorific titles (e.g., the Honorable and Senator) when making reservations, and, as a result, they were not eligible for expedited screening. TSA has a process in place to review and resolve inquiries from passengers who believe they should have received TSA Pre✓™ but did not during a recent travel experience.[70] Although helpful for addressing some TSA Pre✓™-related problems, the process does not provide information on the extent to which TSA is correctly identifying passengers on low-risk lists, because some passengers may not report problems.

TSA's fourth goal (to minimize the number of passengers misidentified as threats on high-risk lists) also addresses system accuracy. The program's related performance measure, its false positive rate, accounts for the number of passengers who have been misidentified as matches to some, but not all, high-risk lists and, thus does not fully assess performance toward the related goal (as shown above, in table 1). TSA's false positive rate does not account for all misidentifications, because, under the current Secure Flight process, TSA has information on passengers misidentified to the No Fly and Selectee Lists, but does not have information on passengers misidentified to the Expanded Selectee or rules-based lists.[71] TSA is currently implementing changes that will allow it to collect more information about passengers misidentified to other

---

[69]Valid Known Traveler Numbers are those that appear on TSA Pre✓™ program lists of passengers eligible for expedited screening.

[70]The process involves TSA's Contact Center, which is staffed with personnel to answer passenger questions or accept passenger feedback about travel-related security screening. Specifically, when passengers submit oral or written feedback that involves failure to receive TSA Pre✓™ screening, a Contact Center representative is to forward this information to Secure Flight. Secure Flight staff investigate these cases to identify and, if necessary, address factors that caused the passenger not to receive TSA Pre✓™ status, such as, for example, mistyping the known travel number or other personal information when making a reservation.

[71]A more detailed explanation of why Secure Flight does not have this information is considered sensitive information and therefore could not be included in a public report.

high-risk lists.[72] This information, if factored into Secure Flight's false positive measure, would allow TSA to more fully assess the program's ability to minimize the misidentification of individuals as potential threats to aviation security.

Measures Addressing Risk-Based Security Capabilities (Goal 5)

TSA does not have any measures that clearly address its goal of incorporating additional risk-based security capabilities to streamline processes and accommodate additional aviation populations (goal 5). According to TSA officials, the goal addresses the program's ability to adapt the Secure Flight system for risk-based screening initiatives, such as TSA Pre✓™ and similar efforts that allow TSA to distinguish high-risk from low-risk passengers. TSA officials identified several measures that address this goal, including program measures for responding to a change in the national threat level, the system false positive rate, and the system availability measure.[73] However, none of the measures TSA identified clearly relate to the goal of adapting the Secure Flight system for different risk-based screening activities, or specify what data should be collected to measure progress toward the goal.

Measures Addressing Privacy (Goal 6)

Secure Flight's privacy-related measure does not allow TSA to fully assess progress toward protecting passenger personal information (goal 6). Upon implementing the program, in January 2009, TSA established privacy protections to, among other things, ensure that personally identifiable information maintained by the Secure Flight system (such as passenger name and date of birth) is properly collected, used, and stored. To assess performance in this area, TSA measures the percentage of passenger records that are purged from the Secure Flight system according to requirements established when the program was

---

[72]According to TSA officials, as of June 2014, Secure Flight had not obtained authorization for additional staff that would be necessary to obtain additional information on misidentifications; therefore, officials were unable to provide a time frame for when these requirements would be implemented.

[73]The Secure Flight system availability measure—a Key Performance Parameter and an OMB 300 Measure—tracks the total amount of time the Secure Flight system (within Secure Flight bounds) is available for matching activities. Secure Flight's false positive measure was discussed previously. All Secure Flight measures are defined in app. III.

implemented.[74] By purging the results of Secure Flight matching and scoring activities from the Secure Flight system, TSA ensures that passenger data do not remain in the system and thus will not be subject to unauthorized use or disclosure. Nevertheless, the measure does not assess other points in time in which the records could be subject to unauthorized use or disclosure, such as before the records are purged or when other government agencies request the results of Secure Flight screening for various purposes, such as an ongoing investigation. When the Secure Flight program was in development, TSA included among a list of possible measures for the fully implemented program a measure for privacy incident compliance (i.e., percentage of privacy incidents reported in compliance with DHS Privacy Incident Handling Guidance). According to TSA officials, since then, TSA has determined that such a measure is not needed because privacy incidents are tracked and publicly reported on at the department level. Nevertheless, additional measures, such as the percentage of government agencies' requests for Secure Flight data that are handled consistently with program privacy requirements, would allow Secure Flight to determine the extent to which the program is appropriately handling passenger information before it is purged from the system.

Secure Flight's performance measures provide program managers some information on its progress with respect to its accuracy-related and privacy-related goals (goals 1 through 4 and 6), but do not measure all aspects of performance critical to achieving these goals. In addition, the measures do not provide information on progress toward the program's risk-based security capabilities goal (goal 5). Additional measures that address key performance aspects related to program goals, and that clearly identify the activities necessary to achieve goals, would allow the program to more fully assess progress toward its goals. For example, the extent to which the Secure Flight system is missing individuals on the No Fly, Selectee, and other high- and low-risk lists is an important dimension

---

[74]These requirements allow Secure Flight to retain Secure Flight matching results for passengers not identified as a match to a government watchlist for up to 7 days, potential matches for up to 7 years, and confirmed matches for up to 99 years, after which they must be purged from the system. According to Secure Flight documentation, records for passengers identified as low risk (either because they match one of the low-risk TSA Pre✓™ Lists or because they were identified as low risk through Secure Flight's flight-by-flight assessments) are treated the same as nonmatches and must be purged within 7 days. Records for passengers who match other watchlists are treated as potential matches and must be purged within 7 years.

of performance related to each of the accuracy-related goals and speaks to a core function of the Secure Flight program—namely to accurately identify passengers on lists. Without measures that provide a more complete understanding of Secure Flight's performance, TSA cannot compare actual with desired results to understand how well the system is achieving these goals. Similarly, without a measure that reflects misidentifications to all high-risk lists, TSA cannot appropriately gauge its performance with respect to its goal of limiting such misidentifications. Likewise, with respect to its privacy-related goal, additional measures that address other key points in the Secure Flight process in which passenger records could be inappropriately accessed would allow Secure Flight to more fully assess the extent to which it is meeting its goal of protecting passenger information. Finally, establishing measures that clearly represent the performance necessary to achieve the program's goal that addresses risk-based security capabilities (goal 5) will allow Secure Flight to determine the extent to which it is meeting its goal of adapting the Secure Flight system for different risk-based screening activities.

TSA Does Not Have Timely and Reliable Information on the Secure Flight System's Matching Errors

TSA does not have timely and reliable information on past Secure Flight system matching errors. As previously discussed, preventing individuals on the No Fly List from boarding an aircraft and identifying individuals on the Selectee List for enhanced screening are key goals of the Secure Flight program. *Standards for Internal Control in the Federal Government* states that agencies must have relevant, reliable, and timely information to determine whether their operations are performing as expected, and that such information can assist agencies in taking any necessary corrective actions to achieve relevant goals.[75] According to TSA officials, when TSA receives information related to matching errors of the Secure Flight system (i.e., the computerized matching and manual reviews conducted to identify matches of passenger and watchlist data), the Match Review Board reviews this information to determine if any actions could be taken to prevent similar errors from happening again. We reviewed meeting minutes and associated documentation for the 51 Match Review Board meetings held from March 2010 through August 2013, and found 16 meetings in which the Match Review Board discussed system matching errors; investigated possible actions to

---

[75]GAO/AIMD-00-21.3.1.

address these errors; and, when possible, implemented changes to strengthen system performance.[76]

However, when we asked TSA for complete information on the extent and causes of system matching errors, we found that TSA does not have readily available or complete information. It took TSA over 6 months to compile a list of such errors, a process that, according to TSA officials, required a significant amount of manual investigation and review.[77] Further, we found that the list was not complete because it did not reflect all system errors that were discussed at the Match Review Board meetings.[78] In addition, we identified in the list TSA provided us discussion of a system error that was not included in the Match Review Board documentation. We also found that, for many incidents on the list, TSA's description of the cause of the error was not sufficiently detailed to understand whether the Secure Flight system was at fault.

Developing a mechanism to systematically document the number and causes of the Secure Flight system's matching errors would provide Secure Flight more timely and reliable information on the extent to which the Secure Flight system is performing as intended. TSA Match Review Board documentation from February, 2012 confirmed the importance of such information, citing the need for more detailed information on instances when the Secure Flight system has not performed as intended. A mechanism to ensure that the results of Match Review Board investigations are systematically documented would be one way to provide such information. Furthermore, without timely and reliable information on system matching errors, TSA is not in the best position to determine whether Secure Flight is achieving relevant goals, investigate

---

[76]We requested documentation for all meetings of the Match Review Board since its implementation in March 2010 through fiscal year 2013, and TSA provided documentation pertaining to 51 meetings. The documentation distributed for meetings included meeting minutes and Power Point slides. The Power Point slides contained detailed information (such as the results of analyses or the status of ongoing work) pertaining to meeting agenda items. More detailed information on performance issues discussed in the meetings is considered sensitive information and cannot be included in a public report.

[77]Information on the time frames of our request and the number of system matching errors TSA identified is considered sensitive information and cannot be included in a public report.

[78]These cases were ones in which the Match Review Board documentation contained sufficient identifying information about Secure Flight system matching errors to allow us to determine it was not included on the list TSA provided us.

all potential causes of these errors, and identify and implement sufficient corrective actions.

Conclusions

The Secure Flight program is one of TSA's key tools for defending civil aviation against terrorist threats. Since TSA began implementing the program, in January 2009, Secure Flight has expanded from a system that matches airline passengers against watchlists of known or suspected terrorists to a system that uses additional high-risk lists and conducts risk-based screening assessments of passengers. Specifically, through the use of new high-risk screening lists, the program now identifies a broader range of high-risk travelers—including ones who may not be on lists of known and suspected terrorists but who nevertheless correspond with known threat criteria. TSA has also begun using Secure Flight to identify low-risk passengers eligible for expedited screening through TSA Pre✓™. Given Secure Flight's importance to securing civil aviation and achieving TSA's risk-based screening goals, the extent to which passengers are being accurately identified by the system (including computerized matching and manual reviews) for standard, expedited, and enhanced screening is critically important. More broadly, to fully realize the security benefits of the Secure Flight program, it is critical that TSA checkpoint personnel correctly identify and appropriately screen travelers according to Secure Flight determinations. Better information on both system and checkpoint performance, therefore, would provide TSA with greater assurance that Secure Flight is achieving its desired purpose to correctly identify passengers for standard, expedited, and enhanced checkpoint screening.

Specifically, TSA would have better assurance that all passengers are screened in accordance with their Secure Flight risk determinations by investigating checkpoint errors and taking appropriate corrective action. Evaluating the root causes of screening errors across all airport checkpoints would provide TSA more complete information on such cases and serve as the basis for policies to ensure the checkpoint is correctly processing passengers. In addition, implementing corrective measures to address the root causes that TSA identifies through its evaluation process would help strengthen checkpoint operations. Furthermore, establishing measures that cover all activities necessary to achieve Secure Flight program goals would allow TSA to more fully assess progress toward these goals. Finally, when TSA learns of Secure Flight system matching errors, a mechanism to systematically document the number and causes of these errors would help ensure that TSA had timely and reliable information to take any corrective action to strengthen system performance.

Recommendations for Executive Action

We recommend that the Transportation Security Administration's Administrator take the following four actions:

- to further improve the implementation of Secure Flight risk determinations at the screening checkpoint, develop a process for regularly evaluating the root causes of screening errors across airports so that corrective measures can be identified;

- to address the root causes of screening errors at the checkpoint, thereby strengthening checkpoint operations, implement the corrective measures TSA identifies through a root cause evaluation process;

- to assess the progress of the Secure Flight program toward achieving its goals, develop additional measures to address key performance aspects related to each program goal, and ensure these measures clearly identify the activities necessary to achieve progress toward the goal; and

- to provide Secure Flight program managers with timely and reliable information on cases in which TSA learns of Secure Flight system matching errors, develop a mechanism to systematically document the number and causes of such cases, for the purpose of improving program performance.

Agency Comments and Our Evaluation

We provided a draft of this report to DHS and the Department of Justice for their review and comment. DHS provided written comments on August 25, 2014, which are summarized below and reproduced in full in appendix IV. DHS concurred with all four of our recommendations and described actions under way or planned to address them. In addition, DHS provided written technical comments, which we incorporated into the report as appropriate.

DHS concurred with our first recommendation, that TSA develop a process for regularly evaluating the root causes of checkpoint screening errors across airports so that corrective measures can be identified. DHS stated that TSA is collecting data on the root causes of checkpoint screening errors in its Security Incident Reporting Tool (SIRT) and that TSA OSO's Operations Performance Division will develop a process for regularly evaluating the root causes of checkpoint screening errors across airports and identify corrective measures. DHS estimates that this will be completed by September 30, 2014. These actions, if implemented effectively, should address the intent of our recommendation.

Regarding our second recommendation, that TSA implement the corrective measures it identifies through a root cause evaluation process, DHS concurred. DHS stated that TSA OSO's Operations Performance Division will evaluate the data gathered from airports through SIRT to identify root causes of checkpoint screening errors and on the basis of the root cause, work with the appropriate TSA program office to implement corrective measures. Such actions could help to reduce the likelihood that TSA will fail to appropriately screen passengers at the screening checkpoint.

Additionally, DHS concurred with our third recommendation, that TSA develop additional measures to address key performance aspects related to each program goal and ensure these measures clearly identify the activities necessary to achieve progress toward the goal. DHS stated that TSA's Office of Intelligence and Analysis will evaluate its current Secure Flight performance goals and measures and develop new performance measures as necessary. DHS further stated that TSA will explore the possibility of implementing analyses to measure match effectiveness through the use of test data sets. Such actions could help TSA better monitor the performance of the Secure Flight program.

DHS also concurred with our fourth recommendation, that TSA develop a mechanism to systematically document the number and causes of cases in which TSA learns that the Secure Flight system has made a matching error. DHS stated that TSA's Office of Intelligence and Analysis will develop a more robust process to track all known cases in which the Secure Flight system has made a matching error, and that the Secure Flight Match Review Board will conduct reviews to identify potential system improvement measures on a quarterly basis. TSA plans to implement these efforts by December 31, 2014. These actions, if implemented effectively, should address the intent of our recommendation. We will continue to monitor DHS's efforts.

The Department of Justice did not have formal comments on our draft report, but provided technical comments, which we incorporated as appropriate.

As agreed with your offices, unless you publicly announce the contents of this report earlier, we plan no further distribution until 30 days from the report date. At that time, we will send copies of this report to the Secretary of Homeland Security, the TSA Administrator, the United States Attorney General, and interested congressional committees as appropriate. In addition, the report will be available at no charge on the GAO website at http://www.gao.gov.

Should you or your staff have any questions about this report, please contact Jennifer A. Grover at 202-512-7141 or groverj@gao.gov. Key contributors to this report are acknowledged in appendix IV. Key points for our Office of Congressional Relations and Public Affairs may be found on the last page of this report.

Jennifer A. Grover
Director
Homeland Security and Justice Issues

Appendix I: Objectives, Scope, and Methodology

This report addresses the following questions:

1. How, if at all, has Secure Flight changed since implementation began in January 2009?

2. To what extent does the Transportation Security Administration (TSA) ensure that Secure Flight screening determinations for passengers are fully implemented at airport security checkpoints?

3. To what extent do TSA's performance measures appropriately assess progress toward achieving the Secure Flight program goals?

To identify how the Secure Flight program has changed since implementation began, we analyzed TSA documentation related to new agency initiatives involving Secure Flight screening since January 2009, including the Secure Flight program concept of operations, privacy notices TSA issued from 2008 (in preparation to begin program implementation) through 2013, and TSA memorandums describing the rationale for new agency initiatives involving the Secure Flight system. We also submitted questions on how Secure Flight has changed to TSA's Office of Chief Counsel and reviewed its responses. To clarify our understanding of a new agency initiative to identify high-risk passengers not already included in the Terrorist Screening Database (TSDB)—the U.S. government's consolidated list of known or suspected terrorists—we spoke with relevant officials in the Intelligence and Analysis Division of TSA's Office of Intelligence and Analysis, who are responsible for the initiative, and with officials from U.S. Customs and Border Protection, who facilitate the generation of one rules-based list. In addition, to understand new initiatives involving Secure Flight screening to identify low-risk travelers, we spoke with Secure Flight program officials and with officials in TSA's Office of Risk Based Security who oversee TSA Pre✓™, a 2011 program that allows TSA to designate preapproved passengers as low risk, and TSA Pre✓™ risk assessments, another initiative to identify passengers as low risk for a specific flight.

To determine the extent to which TSA ensures that the Secure Flight vetting results are fully implemented at airport security checkpoints, we analyzed TSA documents governing the screening checkpoint, such as standard operating procedures for checkpoint screening operations and Travel Document Checkers (TDC) and reviewed reports about the performance of Transportation Security Officers (TSO) at the checkpoint by TSA's Office of Inspections and GAO.[1] To determine the extent to which TSA made errors at the screening checkpoint, we analyzed certain TSA data on TSO performance at the screening checkpoint from May 2012, when TSA began tracking these data, through February 2014, when we conducted the analysis.[2] We examined documentation about these data and interviewed knowledgeable officials, and determined that the data were sufficiently reliable for our purposes. In addition, to clarify our understanding of TSA's checkpoint operations and inform our analysis, we interviewed officials within TSA's Office of Security Operations, which is responsible for checkpoint operations, and TSA officials at nine airports. We selected these nine airports based on a variety of factors, such as volume of passengers screened and geographic dispersion. The results of these interviews cannot be generalized to all airports, but provide insight into TSA's challenges to correctly identify and screen passengers at checkpoints. To better understand how TSA ensures that all passengers have been appropriately screened by Secure Flight, we visited TSA's Identity Verification Call Center to interview officials and observe their identity verification procedures. We compared TSA's checkpoint procedures against *Standards for Internal Control in the Federal Government.*[3] Finally, to determine the extent to which TSA's planned technology solutions could address checkpoint errors, we analyzed documents, such as requests for proposals, related to TSA's planned technology solutions and interviewed knowledgeable TSA officials.

To determine the extent to which Secure Flight performance measures appropriately assess progress toward achieving the program goals, we reviewed documentation of TSA's program goals and performance measures for fiscal years 2012 and 2013—including the measures Secure Flight reports externally to the Department of Homeland Security and the Office of Management and Budget (OMB), as well as other

---

[1]For purposes of this report, and unless otherwise noted, references to TSOs, which include TDCs, include both TSA-employed screening personnel and screening personnel employed by a private sector company contracted with TSA to perform screening services at airports participating in TSA's Screening Partnership Program. See 49 U.S.C. § 44920.

[2]We did not evaluate the extent to which Secure Flight screening determinations for low-risk passengers are implemented at airport security checkpoints. We expect to issue a report on screening for low-risk passengers later this year.

[3]GAO, *Internal Control: Standards for Internal Control in the Federal Government,* GAO/AIMD-00-21.3.1 (Washington, D.C.: Nov. 1, 1999).

internal performance measures Secure Flight officials use for program management purposes—and discussed these measures with Secure Flight officials. We assessed these measures against provisions of the Government Performance and Results Act (GPRA) of 1993 and the GPRA Modernization Act of 2010 requiring agencies to compare actual results with performance goals.[4] Although GPRA's requirements apply at the agency level, in our prior work, we have reported that these requirements can serve as leading practices at lower levels within an organization, such as individual programs or initiatives, through a review of our related products, OMB guidance, and studies by the National Academy of Public Administration and the Urban Institute.[5] We also interviewed relevant TSA officials about the current performance measures for the Secure Flight program and the adequacy of these measures in assessing TSA's progress in achieving program goals.

In addition, to understand how TSA uses Secure Flight-related performance data, we reviewed documentation related to all meetings that TSA identified of the Secure Flight Match Review Board—a multidepartmental entity established to, among other things, review performance measures and recommend changes to improve system performance—from the time was the board was initiated, in March 2010, through August 2013, a total of 51 meetings. To identify the extent to which TSA monitors and evaluates the reasons for any Secure Flight system matching errors, we analyzed a list of such errors that occurred from November 2010 (the point at which the Secure Flight program was implemented for all covered domestic and foreign air carriers) through July 2013 that TSA compiled at our request. To assess the accuracy and completeness of the list TSA provided, we also checked to see if system matching errors we identified in documentation from the Match Review Board meetings were included in TSA's list. We evaluated TSA's efforts to document system matching errors against standards for information and communications identified in GAO's *Standards for Internal Control in the Federal Government*.[6]

---

[4]Government Performance and Results Act of 1993, Pub. L. No. 103-62, 107 Stat. 285 (1993). GPRA was updated by the GPRA Modernization Act of 2010. Pub. L. No. 111-352, 124 Stat. 3866 (2011).

[5]See GAO. *Pipeline Safety: Management of the Office of Pipeline Safety's Enforcement Program Needs Further Strengthening,* GAO-04-801 (Washington, D.C.: July 2004).

[6]GAO/AIMD-00-21.3.1.

We conducted this performance audit from March 2013 to September 2014 in accordance with generally accepted government auditing standards. Those standards require that we plan and perform the audit to obtain sufficient, appropriate evidence to provide a reasonable basis for our findings and conclusions based on our audit objectives. We believe that the evidence obtained provides a reasonable basis for our findings and conclusions.

Appendix II: Secure Flight Screening Lists and Activities

In January 2009, the Transportation Security Administration (TSA) began implementing the Secure Flight program to facilitate the identification of high-risk passengers who may pose security risks to civil aviation, and designate them for additional screening at airport checkpoints. Since then, TSA has begun using Secure Flight to identify low-risk passengers eligible for more efficient processing at the checkpoint. This appendix presents an overview of the lists and other activities as of July 2013 that Secure Flight uses to identify passengers as high risk or low risk.[1] The Secure Flight program, as implemented pursuant to the 2008 Secure Flight Final Rule, requires commercial aircraft operators traveling to, from, within, or overflying the United States to collect information from passengers and transmit that information electronically to TSA.[2] The Secure Flight system uses this information to screen passengers by conducting computerized matching against government lists and other risk assessment activities.[3] As a result of this screening, passengers identified as high risk receive enhanced screening, which includes, in addition to the procedures applied during a typical standard screening experience, a pat-down and either an explosive trace detection search involving a device certified by TSA to detect explosive particles or a physical search of the interior of the passenger's accessible property, electronics, and footwear.[4] Those passengers Secure Flight identifies as low risk are eligible to receive expedited screening, which unlike standard screening, affords travelers certain conveniences, such as not having to remove their belts, shoes, or light outerwear when screened.

---

[1]TSA considers passengers who are not identified by Secure Flight as either low risk or high risk as having unknown risk.

[2]This information, known collectively as Secure Flight Passenger Data (SFPD), includes personally identifiable information, such as full name, gender, date of birth, passport information (if available), and certain nonpersonally identifiable information, such as itinerary information and the unique number associated with a travel record (record number locator). See 49 C.F.R. § 1560.3.

[3]TSA also screens certain nontraveling individuals who are authorized to access the airport's sterile area, such as escorts for minor, elderly, and disabled passengers; airport and aircraft operator employees; and law enforcement officers. In general, the "sterile area" is the portion of an airport beyond the security screening checkpoint that provides passengers access to boarding aircraft and to which access is generally controlled or overseen by TSA. See 49 C.F.R. § 1540.5.

[4]Standard screening typically includes a walk-through metal detector or Advanced Imaging Technology screening, which is to identify objects or anomalies concealed under clothing, and X-ray screening for the passenger's accessible property.

Figure 3 provides information on the lists Secure Flight uses to identify high-risk passengers. Figure 4 describes Secure Flight's activities to identify low-risk passengers, including screening against lists associated with the TSA Pre✓™ Program, a 2011 initiative that allows TSA to designate preapproved passengers as low risk, and TSA Pre✓™ risk assessments, which assess passengers' risk using data submitted to Secure Flight for screening. Figure 5 describes two additional lists Secure Flight uses for passenger screening that, depending on the list, exempt passengers from being designated as low or high risk.

Figure 3: Secure Fight Screening Activities to Identify High-Risk Passengers

Terrorist Screening Database (TSDB) Lists[a]

No Fly List

January 2009
Terrorist Screening Center (TSC)

The No Fly List is a subset of the TSDB containing records of individuals who pose a threat to aviation or national security and are prohibited from boarding an aircraft or entering the sterile area of a U.S. airport.

Selectee List

January 2009
TSC

The Selectee List is a subset of the TSDB containing records of individuals who pose a possible threat to aviation or national security and who are required to undergo enhanced screening at the airport checkpoint prior to entering the airport's sterile area.

Expanded Selectee List

April 2011
TSC

The Expanded Selectee List is a subset of the TSDB. It consists of terrorist records in the TSDB that contain a full name and a full date of birth and meet the reasonable suspicion standard to be considered a known or suspected terrorist, but that do not meet the criteria to be placed on the No Fly or Selectee Lists. Passengers matched to the Expanded Selectee List are to receive enhanced screening at the airport checkpoint prior to entering the airport's sterile area.

High-risk, rules-based lists

Rules-based lists

April 2010 and April 2012
TSA Office of Intelligence and Analysis (OIA)

TSA's rules-based lists include passengers who correspond with certain intelligence-based, high-risk factors, but who may not be in the TSDB. To create the lists, analysts within the Intelligence and Analysis Division of TSA's OIA review current intelligence to identify factors that may indicate an elevated risk for a passenger. TSA creates rules based on these factors and provides them to U.S. Customs and Border Protection (CBP). CBP uses its border screening technology to identify passengers who correspond with the rules and provides TSA information on them in the form of a list. Upon receiving CBP's list, TSA creates a subset of the larger rules-based list, based on additional criteria. Through Secure Flight screening, TSA designates passenger on either rules-based list as selectees for enhanced screening.

Other high-risk lists

Centers for Disease Control and Prevention (CDC) Do Not Board List (DNBL)

Approximately June 2009
CDC

The CDC DNBL includes individuals with communicable diseases who pose a significant health risk to other travelers and, therefore, should not be allowed to fly.

Other activities to identify selectees

Random identification of selectees

June 2010
Secure Flight randomly identifies a certain number of travelers for selectee screening.

Legend

Screening operation → No Fly List

Date incorporated into → 2003
Secure Flight operations → Terrorist Screening Center (TSC)

List owner →

The No Fly List is a subset of the TSDB containing records of individuals who pose a known threat to aviation or national security.

Description →

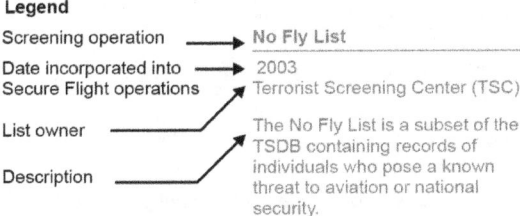

Source: GAO analysis of TSA information. | GAO-14-531

[a]All TSDB-based watchlists utilized by the Secure Flight program contain records determined to meet the Terrorist Screening Center's reasonable suspicion standard. In general, to meet the reasonable suspicion standard, the agency nominating an individual for inclusion in the TSDB must consider the totality of information available that, taken together with rational inferences from that information,

reasonably warrants a determination that an individual is known or suspected to be or have been knowingly engaged in conduct constituting, in preparation for, in aid of, or related to terrorism or terrorist activities. In addition, to be included on the No Fly or Selectee Lists, individuals must meet certain criteria specific to these lists. The TSDB, which is the U.S. government's consolidated watchlist of known or suspected terrorists, also contains records on additional populations of individuals that do not meet the reasonable suspicion standard articulated above but that other federal agencies utilize to support their border and immigration screening missions.

Figure 4: Secure Flight Screening Activities to Identify Low-Risk Passengers

Transportation Security Administration (TSA) Pre✓™ program lists — 5.6 million travelers as of April 2014

The TSA Pre✓™ Program lists offer passengers included on the lists the opportunity to experience expedited screening.

U.S. Customs and Border Protection (CBP) trusted travelers[a]

2,492,962 — October 2011
CBP

A list of individuals enrolled in one of CBP's Trusted Traveler programs (Global Entry, NEXUS, SENTRI) who have undergone a background check and an interview by CBP and who wish to participate in TSA Pre✓™.

National intelligence agencies

70,254 — May 2012
Office of Director of National Intelligence

A list of individuals employed by a national intelligence agency with active Top Secret/Sensitive Compartmentalized Information clearances who wish to participate in TSA Pre✓™.

Federal judges and federal tax court judges

1,308 — June 2012
Administrative Office of the U.S. Courts

A list of federal judges who wish to participate in TSA Pre✓™.

Members of Congress

447 — January 2013
TSA Office of Legislative Affairs

A list of Members of Congress who wish to participate in TSA Pre✓™.

Medal of Honor recipients

79 — February 2013
Congressional Medal of Honor Society

A list of Medal of Honor recipients who wish to participate in TSA Pre✓™.

International Association of Chiefs of Police (IACP)

66 — February 2013
IACP

A list of members of the major U.S. law enforcement associations and other members of the IACP who wish to partcipate in TSA Pre✓™

Homeland Security Advisory Council (HSAC)

14 — August 2013
HSAC

A list of current HSAC members who wish to participate in TSA Pre✓™ HSAC members provide insight and guidance to the DHS Secretary on matters related to homeland security.

Homeland Security Advisors

49 — August 2013
National Governors Association

A list of Homeland Security Advisors (HSA) who wish to participate in TSA Pre✓™. HSAs advise governors of states and territories on homeland security issues.

Department of Defense (DOD) military personnel

2,202,596 — December 2013
DOD

A list of eligible DOD service members, including active duty, National Guard, reserves, and U.S. Coast Guard, who wish to participate in TSA Pre✓™.

TSA Pre✓™ Application Program

180,573 — December 2013
TSA

A list of individuals who apply to the TSA Pre✓™ Application Program to be preapproved as low-risk travelers. TSA conducts a background check to determine if an applicant should be included on this list.

DOD and U.S. Coast Guard civilian employees

700,000 — April 2014
DOD

A list of eligible DOD and U.S. Coast Guard civilian employees who wish to participate in TSA Pre✓™.

Other activities to identify low-risk travelers

TSA Pre✓™ risk assessments

October 2013

TSA risk-based analysis of passenger data submitted to Secure Flight for screening. Data are used to score passengers to identify low-risk passengers who are eligible for expedited screening at the checkpoint.

Legend

◄— Screening operation
◄— Number of travelers in program as of April 2014 and date incorporated into Secure Flight operations
└ List owner
└ Description

Source: GAO analysis of TSA information. | GAO-14-531

[a]In addition to U.S. citizens, the CBP Trusted Traveler Lists also includes U.S. lawful permanent residents and non-U.S. citizen members.

Figure 5: Other Lists Secure Flight Uses for Screening

Additional screening lists

TSA Pre✓™ Disqualification List

26,090   July 2012
TSA Office of Security Operations

The TSA Pre✓™ Disqualification
Protocol List is a watchlist created
and maintained by TSA that
includes individuals who, based
upon their involvement in
violations of security regulations
of sufficient severity or frequency,
are disqualified from receiving
expedited screening for some
period of time or permanently
(e.g., bringing a loaded firearm to
the checkpoint).

TSA Cleared List ◄

135,094   January 2009
TSA-DHS TRIP ◄

The TSA Cleared List is
composed of individuals who
have applied to DHS's Travel
Redress Inquiry Program (DHS
TRIP), and who have been
determined not to be individuals
on the No Fly, Selectee, or
Expanded Selectee Lists, and
who, therefore, should not be
misidentified by Secure Flight as
a match to one of these lists.

Legend

— Screening operation

— Approximate size
(as of February 2014) and
date incorporated into
Secure Flight operations

— List owner

— Description

Source: GAO analysis of TSA information. | GAO-14-531

Appendix III: Secure Flight Performance Data for Fiscal Years 2012 and 2013

This appendix presents data on the Secure Flight program's performance measures and associated performance results that the Transportation Security Administration (TSA) reported externally to the Department of Homeland Security (DHS) and the Office of Management and Budget (OMB). Specifically, table 2 displays data on six Secure Flight Key Performance Parameters—key system capabilities that must be met in order for a system to meet its operational goals—that TSA management reported to DHS for fiscal years 2012 and 2013. Table 3 displays data on five Secure Flight program measures that TSA management reported to OMB for fiscal years 2012 and 2013. The OMB measures are part of the program's yearly exhibit 300, also called the Capital Asset Plan and Business Case, a document that agencies submit to OMB to justify resource requests for major information technology investments.[1] TSA reports performance data for all these measures on a monthly basis, and for each measure, we have provided the range of the performance measurement results for each fiscal year.

Overview of the Secure Flight Screening Process

The Secure Flight program, as implemented pursuant to the 2008 Secure Flight Final Rule, requires commercial aircraft operators traveling to, from, or overflying the United States to collect information from passengers and transmit that information electronically to TSA. This information, known collectively as Secure Flight Passenger Data (SFPD), includes personally identifiable information, such as full name, gender, date of birth, passport information (if available), and certain nonpersonally identifiable information, such as itinerary information and the unique number associated with a travel record (record number locator).[2]

The Secure Flight program designates passengers for risk-appropriate screening by matching SFPD against various lists composed of individuals who should be identified, for the purpose of checkpoint

---

[1]Measures prepared as part of the agency's exhibit 300 are displayed on the Federal Information Technology dashboard website, which was established to provide information on the effectiveness of government information technology programs and to support decisions regarding the investment and management of resources.

[2]See 49 C.F.R. § 1560.3. Aircraft operators must transmit available SFPD to Secure Flight approximately 72 hours prior to scheduled flight departure. For reservations created within 72 hours of flight departure, covered aircraft operators must submit passenger data as soon as they become available.

screening, as either high risk or low risk.[3] With respect to matching passengers against lists, the Secure Flight computer system first conducts automated matching of passenger and watchlist data to identify a pool of passengers who are potential matches to various lists. Next, the system compares all potential matches against the TSA Cleared List, a list of individuals who have applied to, and been cleared through, the DHS redress process.[4] Passengers included on the TSA Cleared List submit a redress number when making a reservation, which allows the Secure Flight system to recognize and clear them.[5] After the system performs automated matching, Secure Flight analysts conduct manual reviews of potential matches to further rule out individuals who are not included on the No Fly and Selectee Lists.

After the completion of manual reviews, TSA precludes passengers who remain potential matches to certain lists from receiving their boarding passes. These passengers, for whom air carriers receive a "passenger inhibited" message from Secure Flight, must undergo a resolution process at the airport. This process may involve air carriers sending updated passenger information back to Secure Flight for automated rematching or placing a call to Secure Flight for assistance in resolving

---

[3]The lists Secure Flight uses to identify high-risk passengers include the No Fly, Selectee, and Expanded Selectee Lists, which are subsets derived from the Terrorist Screening Database, the U.S. government's consolidated watchlist of known or suspected terrorists that is maintained by the Terrorist Screening Center, a multiagency organization administered by the Federal Bureau of Investigation. The lists Secure Flight uses to identify low-risk passengers are associated with the TSA Pre✓™ Program, a 2011 initiative that allows TSA to designate preapproved passengers as low risk. In addition, the system uses passenger data to perform TSA Pre✓™ risk assessments to identify travelers as low risk for a specific flight.

[4]The DHS Traveler Redress Inquiry Program (DHS TRIP) administers the TSA Cleared List. DHS established DHS TRIP in February 2007 to provide individuals, including those who believe they have been delayed or inconvenienced during travel because they have been wrongly identified as the subject of a watchlist record, an opportunity to be cleared. We plan to report later this year on Secure Flight-related redress issues.

[5]Because of the application of other TSA security measures, such as random selection, an individual's presence on the Cleared List will likely diminish, but not preclude, the possibility of being selected for enhanced screening. The technical term for redress number is "redress control number."

the match.[6] At the conclusion of automated and manual screening processes, Secure Flight provides air carriers with a final screening determination for each passenger.[7] At airport checkpoints, those passengers identified as high risk receive enhanced screening and those identified as low risk are eligible for expedited screening.[8]

---

[6]This process may also involve the Secure Flight analyst contacting the Terrorist Screening Center for assistance in confirming or ruling out the match. The Secure Flight Operations Center (SOC) serves as a centralized point for handling the manual review of potential matches, resolving potential matches at the airport, and answering general air carrier questions.

[7]See 49 C.F.R. § 1560.105(b).

[8]Standard screening typically includes a walk-through metal detector or Advanced Imaging Technology screening, which identifies objects or anomalies concealed under clothing, and X-ray screening for the passenger's accessible property. In the event a walk-through metal detector triggers an alarm or the Advanced Imaging Technology identifies an anomaly or suspicious item, additional security measures—such as pat-downs, explosives trace detection searches (which involve a device certified by TSA to detect explosive particles), or additional physical searches—may ensue as part of the resolution process. Enhanced screening includes, in addition to the procedures applied during a typical standard screening experience, a pat-down and an explosives trace detection search or physical search of the interior of the passenger's accessible property, electronics, and footwear. Expedited screening typically includes walk-through metal detector screening and X-ray screening of the passenger's accessible property, but unlike in standard screening, travelers do not have to, among other things, remove their belts, shoes, or light outerwear. Passengers with boarding passes that are not marked for enhanced or expedited screening receive standard screening, unless otherwise identified by TSA for enhanced or expedited screening through the application of random and unpredictable security measures at the screening checkpoint.

Table 2: Secure Flight Key Performance Parameters and Results for Fiscal Years 2012 and 2013

Goal	Definition	Threshold[a]	Objective[b]	Range for 2012	Range for 2013
Program response time to a change in threat level	Secure Flight's ability to adjust the Secure Flight system and appropriately staff the Secure Flight Operations Center (SOC) to match a change in threat level[c]	48 hours	24 hours	24 hours[d]	Not applicable[e]
Resolution Service Center service level	The percentage of phone calls to the SOC that are answered in 10 seconds or less	88%	90%	79.73% to 97.51%[f]	94.85% to 98.03%
Secure Flight system match rates (domestic)	The estimated match rates by the Secure Flight system under normal operating circumstances, assuming that the passenger information provided includes full name and date of birth	0.125%	<=0.1%	0.08% to 0.12%	0.07% to 0.09%
False positive rate	The percentage of passengers whose name is deemed a match after being processed through the Secure Flight name-matching processing, including identification verification	0.06%	0.03%	0.0015% to 0.0023%	0.0017% to 0.0026%
Service availability[g]	The total percentage of time the system is up and running[h]	99.95%	99.99%	99.98% to 100%[i]	100%[j]
Automated clearing of redressed individuals[k]	The percentage of redressed individuals automatically cleared by Secure Flight who have submitted a redress number that is on the Transportation Security Administration (TSA) Cleared List	98%	99.99%	99.57% to 99.99%	99.78% to 99.99%

Source: GAO analysis of Transportation Security Administration data. | GAO-14-531

[a]According to Secure Flight officials, the threshold represents the minimum acceptable performance for the parameter.

[b]According to Secure Flight officials, the objective represents Secure Flight's desired level of performance for the parameter.

[c]The Department of Homeland Security National Terrorism Advisory System is to communicate information about the risk of a terrorist attack on the United States by providing timely, detailed information to the public, government agencies, first responders, airports and other transportation hubs, and the private sector. Using available information, the Secretary of Homeland Security will make a statement to indicate that there has been a change in the threat level. These alerts are to provide a clear statement that there is an imminent threat or an elevated threat.

[d]There was one change in threat level during fiscal year 2012, and in response to that change, Secure Flight met its performance objective.

[e]According to TSA officials, there are no performance data for this measure for fiscal year 2013 because there was no change in the national threat level during this period.

[f]Secure Flight did not meet its performance threshold or objective for Resolution Service Center Service Level for 1 month during fiscal year 2012. According to a TSA official, there was a high number of airline system outages reported to the SOC for multiple airlines, which caused an unexpected workload increase.

[g]Secure Flight also tracks service availability as one of its Office of Management and Budget (OMB)-reported measures (see table 3).

[h]The percentage is derived from a 12-month rolling average.

[i]Secure Flight did not meet its performance objective for service availability for 2 months in fiscal year 2012.

[j]Performance results were 100 percent throughout fiscal year 2013.

[k]Secure Flight also tracks automated clearing of redressed individuals as one of its OMB-reported measures (see table 3).

Table 3: Secure Flight Office of Management and Budget (OMB) Performance Measures and Results for Fiscal Years 2012 and 2013

Measure	Definition	Performance target	Range for 2012	Range for 2013
Percentage of aircraft operators on-boarded with Secure Flight	The percentage of aircraft operators on-boarded with Secure Flight of all aircraft operators covered by the Secure Flight final rule	100%	100%[a]	100%[a]
Automated clearing of redressed individuals[b]	The percentage of redressed individuals automatically cleared by Secure Flight who have submitted a redress number that is on the Transportation Security Administration (TSA) Cleared List	95%	99.57% to 99.99%	99.78% to 99.99%
Percentage of records purged in accordance with National Archives and Records Administration schedule retention guidelines[c]	The percentage of records purged of those records scheduled to be purged	100%	100%[d]	100%[d]
Service availability[e]	The total monthly minutes of Secure Flight system availability minus the total duration in minutes of significant Secure Flight system disruptions, divided by total monthly availability of Secure Flight in minutes	99.99%	99.98% to 100%[f]	100%[g]
Compliant Secure Flight Passenger Data (SFPD) submissions	The percentage of air carrier submissions that include the passenger's full name, date of birth, and gender (i.e., the key passenger data required for Secure Flight screening)	100%	97.24% to 97.88%[h]	97.44% to 99.96%[h]

Source: GAO analysis of TSA data. | GAO-14-531

[a]Performance results were 100 percent for each month of the fiscal year.

[b]Secure Flight also tracks automated clearing of redress individuals as one of its Key Performance Parameters (see table 2). According to Secure Flight officials, the Key Performance Parameter objective and the OMB 300 performance target should not be different for this measure.

[c]In implementing Secure Flight, TSA established privacy protections to, among other things, ensure that personally identifiable information maintained by the Secure Flight system, such as passenger name and date of birth, is properly collected, used, and stored. Specifically, the requirements allow Secure Flight to store results for passengers not identified as a match to a government watchlist for up to 7 days, potential matches for up to 7 years, and confirmed matches for 99 years, after which they must be purged from the system. According to Secure Flight documentation, records for passengers identified as low risk are treated the same as nonmatches and must be purged within 7 days. Records for passengers who match the Expanded Selectee and rules-based lists are treated as potential matches and must be purged within 7 years.

[d]Performance results were 100 percent throughout the fiscal year.

[e]Secure Flight also tracks service availability as one of its Key Performance Parameters (see table 2).

[f]Secure Flight did not meet its performance target for service availability for 2 months during the fiscal year.

[g]Performance results were 100 percent throughout fiscal year 2013.

[h]Secure Flight did not meet its performance target for any month during this fiscal year. Secure Flight officials stated that this metric is outside of the program's control because Secure Flight relies on air carriers to submit these data. According to TSA officials, to improve air carrier compliance, TSA monitors carrier submissions and works with carriers to inform them about Secure Flight data requirements.

U.S. Department of Homeland Security
Washington, DC 20528

August 25, 2014

Jennifer A. Grover
Director, Homeland Security and Justice Issues
U.S. Government Accountability Office
441 G Street, NW
Washington, DC 20548

Re: Draft Report GAO-14-531, "SECURE FLIGHT: TSA Should Take Additional Steps to
   Determine Program Effectiveness"

Dear Ms. Grover:

Thank you for the opportunity to review and comment on this draft report. The U.S. Department
of Homeland Security (DHS) appreciates the U.S. Government Accountability Office's (GAO's)
work in planning and conducting its review and issuing this report.

As highlighted in this report, Secure Flight is a frontline defense against terrorism targeting the
Nation's civil aviation system. Secure Flight has been a very effective tool in identifying
individuals who should not be allowed to board commercial aircraft, should receive enhanced
screening prior to boarding an aircraft, or who should be given expedited screening.

The draft contained four recommendations with which the Department concurs. Specifically,
GAO recommended that the Transportation Security Administration (TSA) Administrator:

Recommendation 1: Develop a process for regularly evaluating the root causes of screening
errors across airports so that corrective measures can be identified.

Response: Concur. The TSA Office of Security Operations, Operations Performance Division,
will develop a process for regularly evaluating the root causes of screening errors across airports
and identify corrective measures. TSA is collecting data on the root causes of screening errors in
its Security Incident Reporting Tool (SIRT). SIRT collects the following data regarding each
identified screening error: root cause, corrective action implemented locally, date implemented,
name of verifying official, date verified, additional root cause comments, corrective action
comments, and lessons learned-preventative actions. Estimated Completion Date (ECD):
September 30, 2014.

Recommendation 2: Implement the corrective measures TSA identifies through a root cause evaluation process.

Response: Concur. The TSA Office of Security Operations, Operations Performance Division, will evaluate the data gathered from airports through SIRT to identify root causes of screening errors and based on the root cause, work with the appropriate TSA program office to implement appropriate corrective measures. ECD: To Be Determined (TBD).

Recommendation 3: Develop additional measures to address key performance aspects related to each program goal, and ensure these measures clearly identify the activities necessary to achieve progress toward the goal.

Response: Concur. TSA's Office of Intelligence and Analysis will evaluate its current Secure Flight performance goals and measures and will develop new performance measures as necessary. Specifically, for Secure Flight performance goals 1 through 4, TSA will explore the possibility of implementing analyses to measure match effectiveness through the use of test data sets.

Secure Flight performance goal 5 addresses Secure Flight's ability to incorporate additional risk-based security capabilities to streamline processes and accommodate additional aviation populations. TSA will review current performance measures and make adjustments as deemed appropriate for this goal.

Secure Flight performance goal 6, TSA has control measures in-place that address key points in the Secure Flight process such as: robust security implemented in the Secure Flight system; access restriction to approved, authorized users; badge-controlled access; account lockouts after unsuccessful attempts to access a system; and, audit logs and other physical and technical controls. TSA has also implemented administrative control measures such as privacy awareness training, privacy rules of behavior, and a formal system access approval process before access is granted.

TSA has implemented a process for handling requests for Secure Flight data that has been documented in TSA Management Directive (MD) 1300.4, Requests for Secure Flight Data. TSA will implement a tracking mechanism for requests and their disposition under MD1300.4. ECD: July 31, 2015.

Recommendation 4: Develop a mechanism to systematically document the number and causes of such cases for the purpose of improving program performance.

Response: Concur. Currently, the Secure Flight Match Review Board selectively reviews Secure Flight system matching errors when technical changes to Secure Flight's matching logic can likely prevent similar errors in the future. TSA's Office of Intelligence and Analysis will develop a more robust process to track all instances in which Secure Flight becomes aware of Secure Flight system matching errors. The Match Review Board will conduct reviews to identify potential improvement measures on a quarterly basis. ECD: December 31, 2014.

2

Again, thank you for the opportunity to review and provide comments on this draft report. Technical comments were previously provided under separate cover. Please feel free to contact me if you have any questions. We look forward to working with you in the future.

Sincerely,

Jim H. Crumpacker, CIA, CFE
Director
Departmental GAO-OIG Liaison Office

3

Appendix V: GAO Contact and Staff Acknowledgments

GAO Contact	Jennifer A. Grover, 202-512-7141, groverj@gao.gov
Staff Acknowledgments	In addition to the contact named above, Maria Strudwick (Assistant Director), Mona Nichols Blake (Analyst-in-Charge), John de Ferrari, Michele Fejfar, Imoni Hampton, Eric Hauswirth, Susan Hsu, Richard Hung, Justine Lazaro, Benjamin Licht, Tom Lombardi, Linda Miller, David Plocher, and Ashley Vaughan made key contributions to this report.

GAO's Mission	The Government Accountability Office, the audit, evaluation, and investigative arm of Congress, exists to support Congress in meeting its constitutional responsibilities and to help improve the performance and accountability of the federal government for the American people. GAO examines the use of public funds; evaluates federal programs and policies; and provides analyses, recommendations, and other assistance to help Congress make informed oversight, policy, and funding decisions. GAO's commitment to good government is reflected in its core values of accountability, integrity, and reliability.
Obtaining Copies of GAO Reports and Testimony	The fastest and easiest way to obtain copies of GAO documents at no cost is through GAO's website (http://www.gao.gov). Each weekday afternoon, GAO posts on its website newly released reports, testimony, and correspondence. To have GAO e-mail you a list of newly posted products, go to http://www.gao.gov and select "E-mail Updates."
Order by Phone	The price of each GAO publication reflects GAO's actual cost of production and distribution and depends on the number of pages in the publication and whether the publication is printed in color or black and white. Pricing and ordering information is posted on GAO's website, http://www.gao.gov/ordering.htm.
	Place orders by calling (202) 512-6000, toll free (866) 801-7077, or TDD (202) 512-2537.
	Orders may be paid for using American Express, Discover Card, MasterCard, Visa, check, or money order. Call for additional information.
Connect with GAO	Connect with GAO on Facebook, Flickr, Twitter, and YouTube. Subscribe to our RSS Feeds or E-mail Updates. Listen to our Podcasts. Visit GAO on the web at www.gao.gov.
To Report Fraud, Waste, and Abuse in Federal Programs	Contact: Website: http://www.gao.gov/fraudnet/fraudnet.htm E-mail: fraudnet@gao.gov Automated answering system: (800) 424-5454 or (202) 512-7470
Congressional Relations	Katherine Siggerud, Managing Director, siggerudk@gao.gov, (202) 512-4400, U.S. Government Accountability Office, 441 G Street NW, Room 7125, Washington, DC 20548
Public Affairs	Chuck Young, Managing Director, youngc1@gao.gov, (202) 512-4800 U.S. Government Accountability Office, 441 G Street NW, Room 7149 Washington, DC 20548

Please Print on Recycled Paper.

www.ingramcontent.com/pod-product-compliance
Lightning Source LLC
Chambersburg PA
CBHW080541290526
45790CB00006B/2502